TRANSFORMATIVE CHURCH PLANTING MOVEMENT

Let the Journey Begin

MARTIN LEO JONES

DEDICATION

This book is dedicated my best friend, partner, and editor-in-chief
– my wife, Karen. She continually encouraged me to put my
thoughts on paper, partly because she saw the value of them and
partly because she was tired of hearing them. She is the backboard
for bouncing my ideas off of, the filter for straining my rubbish,
and the sandpaper to knock off my rough edges. Outside of God,
she knows how I think and what I am thinking better than anyone
on this earth. She is one of the smartest people I know and knows
me better than anyone and still hangs out with me. She has been
one of the greatest expressions of God's grace to me for 30+ years
as my wife and the mother of my children. I love you, Karen.

CONTENTS

Acknowledgments   vii

1   POWER OF A COMMA   1

2   THE NEED FOR A NEW PARADIGM   6

3   TRADITIONAL OR NEW TESTAMENT THINKING?   13

4   PARADIGM SHIFT: SHIFT TO WHAT?   23

5   UNDERSTANDING TCPM   35

6   BIBLICAL BASIS FOR TCPM   40

7   THE BASIC FRACTAL OF TCPM   46

8   THE BASIC FRACTAL OF TCPM: GO TO BAPTIZE, BAPTIZE TO TEACH, TEACH TO GO   56

9   GO TO BAPTIZE: TRANSFORMATIVE CALLING   62

10   BAPTIZE TO TEACH: TRANSFORMATIVE RELATIONSHIPS   68

11   TEACH TO GO: TRANSFORMATIVE WORD OF GOD   72

12   TCPM ORGANIZATION   86

13   CONCLUSION   90

ACKNOWLEDGMENTS

I admit that this book would not be possible without the people that God has placed in my life to love and serve. Like the gravitational pull of a planet against a meteor, God has placed them in my life as He has seen fit to tweak my course and change my direction. I am a product of my relationships the good ones and the not so good ones. These people would include family, friends, parishioners, and pastors. Because I am so cheap and these pages so expensive, I cannot name you all. All I can say is: you know who you are and thanks for all the pulls and nudges that kept me on course.

MARTIN LEO JONES

CHAPTER 1

POWER OF A COMMA

What a difference a comma makes. Consider Ephesians 4:11-12. As you read the passages below and compare the translations, pay close attention to the comma after the word "saints" in verse 12.

Ephesians 4:11–12 (NKJV) [11] *And He Himself gave some to be apostles, some prophets, some evangelists, and some pastors and teachers,* [12] *for the equipping of the <u>saints for</u> the work of ministry, for the edifying of the body of Christ,*

Ephesians 4:11–12 (KJV 1900) [11] *And he gave some, apostles; and some, prophets; and some, evangelists; and some, pastors and teachers;* [12] *For the perfecting of the <u>saints, for</u> the work of the ministry, for the edifying of the body of Christ:*

The impact of the comma after the word "saints" in verse 12 is descriptive of the struggle that we as pastors and leaders have faced for many years. The comma in the 1900 KJV indicates three separate responsibilities for pastors and leaders, one of those being to do the work of the ministry. On the other hand, the NKJV says that leadership exists to equip saints so THEY can do ministry. While the pastors and leaders would prefer the NKJV, that God has given leadership *for the equipping of the saints for the work of ministry*, the church functions more with the comma in place, like the KJV 1900 edition, where pastors and leaders exist for *the perfecting of the saints, [and] for the work of the ministry.*

While we believe that every Christian should be a minister--that all who have been reconciled to God have the ministry of reconciliation (2 Corinthians 5:17-21), the church seems to function quite differently, with the few doing most of the reconciling and the rest just watching. It seems the church is stuck in the 80/20 rule with 80% of the people doing 20% of the work while 20% of the people do 80% of the work. This may even be too generous for many of the ministries I have been a part of and now serve. The pastor and his wife do most of the work.

> **...life-long ministries are consumed by efforts to get people out of the stands and onto the field.**

Instead of the fully armed warriors described in Ephesians 6 on the battlefield battling evil with God's word and faith, our churches seemed to be filled with spectators and fans watching the battle from a safe distance, rooting for God and good to vanquish evil. How many pastors, seeing the great need that lostness creates, envision a church filled with participants investing their lives in the work of God, only to be shocked and disappointed by the reality of the mediocrity of the masses? While these leaders see the world as a battlefield for soldiers (saints), the churches they serve often see it as an arena for gladiators (ministers) with them as the spectators. As a result, life-long ministries are consumed by efforts to get people out of the stands and onto the field.

The question is, "The 80/20 rule, whose fault is it?" While most of us in leadership would like to blame the lack of spiritual growth and maturity on parishioners, many parishioners may say they are not inspired or challenged to participate. Maybe the problem is bigger than both. Maybe it is inherent in our processes, systems, and traditions. Could it be that we have created or inherited styles, systems, programs, and ways of doing things that are perfect for getting what we are getting, i.e., lack of participation? Years ago I read a book by Norman Wright in which he talked about the power of non-verbals in good communication. He stated that only 10% of what we communicate was content or the actual words we say, and that 35% was in our tone of voice or the way we say things, while 55% of our communication is nonverbal or what we are doing when we are saying it. This information changed my life and really helped my marriage. Because of it, I have learned how to tell Karen, my wife, I love her with a dishwasher, vacuum, washer and dryer. When I am at the sink rinsing dishes, putting them in the dishwasher, and tell her I love her, she will tell you that she gets it. It is through consistent acts of service (nonverbals), such as laundry and dishwashing, and the environment they create that my words have meaning.

I have learned that nonverbals are a major player in all communication, including what we are doing or the environment we create as we strive to communicate in church. While we want to communicate that we want and need greater participation, our nonverbals such as our architecture, setup, programs, what we are doing and the way we are doing it, may be saying "Just sit, watch and listen." For example, auditoriums have two main areas: the stage and the floor. The stage is where the majority of the action takes place while the floor is where action takes place only by invitation. The stage is in complete control of the floor, and participation is discouraged outside of permission. In this setting it would be awkward for someone to stand and say, "I have a question" or "I am not sure I understand" or even more awkward for someone to get personal and say, "This is me you're talking about. Can we stop and pray for me?" 1 Corinthians 14 seems to suggest that people should have the privilege and are even expected to participate as long as it is done in an orderly manner.

26 What then shall we say, brothers and sisters? When you come together, each of you has a hymn, or a word of instruction, a revelation, a tongue or an interpretation. Everything must be done so that the church may be built up. 27 If anyone speaks in a tongue, two—or at the most three—should speak, one at a time, and someone must interpret. 28 If there is no interpreter, the speaker should keep quiet in the church and speak to himself and to God. 29 Two or three prophets should speak, and the others should weigh carefully what is said. 30 And if a revelation comes to someone who is sitting down, the first speaker should stop. 31 For you can all prophesy in turn so that everyone may be instructed and encouraged. 32 The spirits of prophets are subject to the control of prophets. 33 For God is not a God of disorder but of peace— as in all the congregations of the Lord's people. (1 Corinthians 14:26- 33, NIV)

In a large group, it would be anarchy if everyone in the church service was allowed and felt the freedom to speak publicly. Thus, a larger group demands a stronger role of leadership and greater efficiency. The problem is efficiency does not equal effectiveness. When you add to this the fact that our Sunday service, with the nonverbals of spectating and not participating, is the big event of the week, it may be we are getting what we are literally set up to get – an audience and performers. All of this is based on our present way of thinking of church as a large unit and putting its corresponding needs in the driver's seat.

But!!!! What if we were willing to change the way we think about church? What if small, fully functioning reproductive units were as natural as large gatherings? What if a circle of a few was more intrinsic to us than the one to many, the stage to the floor, of a large gathering? What if smaller units in smaller venues where participation is encouraged and service is expected were standard practice? Could it be that the nonverbals of a small room of 20 without stage separation is far more conducive to great participation and involvement in ministry? This is worth thinking about and we shall!

How about we rethink everything, confident that if our ideas are truth, then they will stand up to scrutiny? If something is God's truth, it is as He is, immovable, unshakable, and firm as a rock. This truth applies to all ways of man's thinking, including this Transformative Church Planting Movement Preview. This preview is created to be an alternative, an option, but not an exact prescription. As I said before, if there is truth, it will hold up. My desire is that each reader determines what is applicable and beneficial, whether the whole or in part. I am even willing for you to reject it totally, so why not consider a new way of looking at church, a new paradigm?

CHAPTER 2

THE NEED FOR A NEW PARADIGM

par·a·digm (păr'ə-dīm', -dĭm') n. A set of assumptions, concepts, values, and practices that constitute a way of viewing reality for the community that shares them.

A paradigm refers to a person's way of thinking by which information is filtered, producing attitudes, beliefs, behaviors, habits, and traditions. These traditions are often instinctive, reactionary, and unconscious. A paradigm is the box in "thinking outside the box." Paradigms are often expressed in one-word descriptions we use to convey our understanding about the worldview of others. We might say people are "lost," "worldly," or "pagan," meaning they are thinking and behaving in such a way. Paradigms are powerful. Wars are fought over paradigms. Religions are formed around group paradigms.

> **A paradigm is the box in "thinking outside the box."**

Biblical Christianity continually calls us to challenge our paradigms, mostly because we believe that in this life we are always in process or on a journey moving from one state to another. We call this journey "sanctification" or being made holy like God our Father. It is only by the grace of God through Christ's work that we can even engage this journey. The truth is Christianity should in and of itself be a continual paradigm shift changing the way we think, see, feel, and act, making us more like Christ.

2 Corinthians 5:17 (NKJV) 17 Therefore, if anyone is in Christ, he is a new creation; old things have passed away; behold, all things have become new.

Romans 12:1-2 Therefore, I urge you, brothers and sisters, in view of God's mercy, to offer your bodies as a living sacrifice, holy and pleasing to God—this is your true and proper worship. 2 Do not conform to the pattern of this world, but be transformed by the renewing of your mind. Then you will be able to test and approve what God's will is—his good, pleasing and perfect will.

The Christian's paradigm should be that we are new creations continually in a state of transformation. When we lose sight of this, we stop God's process of sanctification.

ILLUSTRATION OF A PARADIGM SHIFT: FEEL THE PAIN

I know people for whom driving makes them angry--good people for whom getting behind the wheel turns them into demons, with drivers around them always moving too slow or too fast or too close or too far away. I am not generally one of those drivers, but there are two things that seem to get, as my mother would say, stuck in my craw. While I get angry when someone is following me too closely, I get irate when someone cuts me off. Maybe it comes from all the bullies who cut in the lunch line when I was a kid. The scars remain; cutting in line makes me mad. I know I am not the only one.

Imagine with me that you are about to pull onto the expressway, and as you are waiting for your opening to merge left into traffic, the car behind you changes lanes, takes your opening, and cuts you off. Are you feeling what I am feeling right now? What makes it worse is that the driver who did this to you is now right ahead of you and is signaling to get off at the next exit. Are you feeling more of what I am feeling? Stop and remember you are a Christian. Although you are not allowed to yell or display obscenities, you can get beside them and give them "the look." Although you would never tell them to "go to hell," you can with "the look" remind them that it is actions like these that are the reasons they may be going there. So as they are slowing down to exit the expressway, you see your opportunity to pull beside them to give them the "Oh yes, you are going to hell" look.

STOP HERE. ANSWER THE FOLLOWING QUESTIONS:

- What happened?
- What are the facts?
- What did you see or perceive?
- What did you observe beyond the facts?
- Who did you identify with?
- How do you feel about the driver?
- What should have been done?
- What does this say about character of the driver?

STORY CONTINUED:

As you pull beside this wretched sinner, who in one act has proven the total depravity of man, as you are matching your speed to his in a way that he should notice and look your direction, and just as you are prepared to give him "the look," you notice the woman sitting next to him who appears to have a basketball under her shirt and is breathing very heavily through her mouth as though she has just run a mile. You then notice the young male driver with a death grip on the steering wheel like a NASCAR racer. Then you look up and see the hospital sign at the next exit. All of a sudden it hits you that this couple is having a baby. SOON!

STOP AGAIN AND ANSWER THE FOLLOWING QUESTIONS:

- In what ways did the facts change?
- How did your perception change?
- Who do you identify with now?
- How did your feelings change?
- What could be done differently?
- What would you say about this driver now?
- Did you experience a paradigm shift?

Chances are, on a small level, you experienced a paradigm shift. When the facts changed and you saw the clear truth of the situation, your perception changed. If you are a father, you quickly identified with the driver, and to you this demon-possessed, reckless driver became a soon-to-be father. If you are like me, in a split second I went from anger to sympathy, and I went from wanting to rebuke to wanting to help any way I could. My opinion of the character of the driver went from reckless young man to caring, expectant father. A paradigm shift changes the way I think, see, feel, do, and am.

PARADIGM SHIFT BETWEEN ACTS 1 AND ACTS 2

Acts 1:4-11 On one occasion, while he was eating with them, he gave them this command: "Do not leave Jerusalem, but wait for the gift my Father promised, which you have heard me speak about. 5 For John baptized with water, but in a few days you will be baptized with the Holy Spirit." 6 Then they gathered around him and asked him, "Lord, are you at this time going to restore the kingdom to Israel?" 7 He said to them: "It is not for you to know the times or dates the Father has set by his own authority. 8 But you will receive power when the Holy Spirit comes on you; and you will be my witnesses in Jerusalem, and in all Judea and Samaria, and to the ends of the earth." 9 After he said this, he was taken up before their very eyes, and a cloud hid him from their sight. 10 They were looking intently up into the sky as he was going, when suddenly two men dressed in white stood beside them. 11 "Men of Galilee," they said, "why do you stand here looking into the sky? This same Jesus, who has been taken from you into heaven, will come back in the same way you have seen him go into heaven." (NIV)

Jesus battled the paradigm of the first century Messiah. It seems like the whole of Israel had forgotten every Old Testament passage concerning the suffering Messiah and could only see the Triumphant Messiah. The world of Jesus was looking for a King David-like Messiah who would defeat Rome and establish the Kingdom of Israel as the ruling class of the world. The idea of a suffering Messiah, who would defeat the greater foe of sin and death and establish God's kingdom in the hearts of men, was not even on their radar.

> **They wanted more than healing and raising the dead; they wanted Jesus to show them aggressive displays of power.**

Every miracle of Jesus was filtered through this King David paradigm. Feeding the 5000 meant that their troops would have no need to maintain supply lines as they marched on Rome.

Every miracle of Jesus was filtered through their "restore the kingdom to Israel" paradigm. If the Israelite soldiers died on the battlefield, Jesus could simply speak the words and resurrect His whole army to fight another day. I have often wondered why the Jewish leaders, in the midst of all the miracles Jesus performed, continually asked Him to prove Himself with a sign. Why weren't the miraculous signs He performed sufficient for them to believe? It is because they were looking for offensive signs, not just defensive ones. They wanted more than healing and raising the dead; they wanted Jesus to show them aggressive displays of power. "Jesus, don't just heal people. Kill a few Romans to show us you are the Messiah." This was what they wanted.

Jesus' disciples were so embedded in this same paradigm, they rejected every attempt that Jesus made to change it. This paradigm led them to be confused and even opposed anytime Jesus spoke of His death and departure from this earth, even at times rebuking Him for such thinking (Matthew 16:22). "Lord, are you at this time going to restore the kingdom to Israel?" is a post resurrection statement demonstrating that His disciples were still locked into this paradigm, more interested in their kingdom than His. They were dumbfounded by Jesus' ascension; at the time they thought He should be gathering His army, He was leaving. This is why they were looking intently (staring) into the sky as Jesus departed. It took two angels to break them up and get them to do what Jesus had told them to do in Acts 1:4: Go back to Jerusalem and wait for the Holy Spirit.

The life, teachings, death, and resurrection of Jesus could not change the paradigm of the disciples. It could only be changed through the gracious gift of the Holy Spirit in Acts 2. Upon the Spirit's arrival, everything changed from the inside out. After Pentecost they were no longer interested in defeating Rome and restoring Israel; they were now interested in defeating sin and glorifying the reigning Christ. After Pentecost they were ready to fulfill the Great Commission (Matthew 28:18-20) motivated by the Great Commandment (Matthew 22:37-40) all the way to the ends of the earth (Acts 1:8).

Is this not true today? Being a Christian is a continual paradigm shift that requires the life, teachings, death, burial, and resurrection of Jesus and, especially, the work of the Holy Spirit. You cannot be filled with the Spirit without a paradigm shift, without Him challenging the way you presently think, see, feel, act, and are. Biblical Christianity is a paradigm shift where the Spirit reaches into the core of our being, making internal changes, which are outwardly observed.

A movement of God is all about a paradigm shift. Biblically and throughout history, the greatest opposition to the movement of God has been the paradigms of the religious community and the traditions that support them. Jesus was rejected because of the King David/Messiah paradigm and all the traditions that surrounded it. Just like many religious people, they were good at taking a little of God and His word and mixing it with traditions and calling it godly.

CHAPTER 3

TRADITIONAL OR NEW TESTAMENT THINKING?

After graduating seminary I planted my second church, and after two years we grew from about 10 to 60 and built our first building. It would have been a success story except for one thing: I was burned out. As we erected the building, I became a wreck. While I was preaching "live by faith," I was living by sight. Worry and fear of interim interest, city code compliance, and weather were my constant companions. While I was telling everyone things were great, I was falling apart. It all came to a head one morning. After arriving at my office, my new office in my new church building, I was sitting at my desk when a sadness gripped me so tightly that I spent the whole morning staring at the wall, weeping like a baby. I do not cry very much, but I could not stop crying on that day. I knew something was the matter, so I called a counselor I knew. Although I did not know him very well, I was willing to talk to anyone to get help. When I called him, all I could say was, "Roy, I just spent the last 3 hours staring at the wall and crying like a baby. Something's the matter." He responded, "I would say so. Why don't you meet me for breakfast in the morning?" So I did, and, over the next few weeks, Roy taught me about burnout and about me.

> ...burnout was a million dollar experience. I would not take a million dollars for what it taught me, but I would not take a million to go through it again either.

I ended up leaving the ministry and going to prison...oh yes, to work in a prison as a teacher and later as a chaplain. God, over the next two years, used the Federal Bureau of Prisons to teach me about Him, myself, and others. My burnout was a million dollar experience. I would not take a million dollars for what it taught me, but I would not take a million to go through it again either. One thing it taught me was that my paradigm, or the way that I viewed ministry and the world, was a major contributor to my burnout. Remember: a paradigm refers to a person's way of thinking by which information is filtered, producing attitudes, beliefs, behaviors, habits, and traditions. These traditions are often instinctive, reactive, and unconscious.

Tradition was a major part of the paradigm that led to my burnout. I believed that in order to be a church you had to look like a church and act like a church. So I started my church with a traditional weekly schedule: Sunday School at 9:45, Worship at 11, Church Training at 6, Sunday Evening Worship at 7 PM, Tuesday Night visitation, and, of course, Wednesday Night Prayer Meeting and Bible Study. Oh yes, allow me to throw into the mix regular 6 AM men's prayer time, counseling, pastoral care and visitation of members. and, being a church plant, regular door to door prospecting. This schedule came from my traditions which came from the way I was raised and trained; it was the way that I viewed my world; it was my paradigm.

In the second year of the church plant, the school we had been meeting in told us we needed to move out because they needed to expand. Because there was literally nowhere else to hold church in this young community, we decided to build our own building. This was OK with me because a building was a tradition completing my paradigm. With a building and all these activities, we would look like a church and act like a church and thus be a church.

> **Most of us started ministry with a paradigm that was filled with unnecessary traditions that took a lot of pain to let go of.**

Looking back today, I can clearly see the many "essentials" of my tradition that in reality were unnecessary. It was my need to meet these "essentials" that led to my emotional bankruptcy. In my experience, I have found that my journey is the same as many other pastors. Most of us started ministry with a paradigm that was filled with unnecessary traditions that took a lot of pain to let go of.

JESUS AND TRADITION

*Matthew 15:1-9 (NIV) Then some Pharisees and teachers of the law came to Jesus from Jerusalem and asked, 2"Why do your disciples **break** the tradition of the elders? They don't wash their hands before they eat!" 3 Jesus replied, "And why do you **break** the command of God for the sake of your tradition? 4For God said, 'Honor your father and mother' and 'Anyone who curses their father or mother is to be put to death.' 5But you say that if anyone declares that what might have been used to help their father or mother is 'devoted to God,' 6they are not to 'honor their father or mother' with it. Thus you **nullify** the word of God for the sake of your tradition. 7You hypocrites! Isaiah was right when he prophesied about you: 8" 'These people honor me with their lips, but their hearts are far from me. 9They worship me in vain; their teachings are merely human rules.' "*

Although Jesus never violated the law of the Old Testament, He didn't mind messing with the traditions of the Pharisees, especially those that prevented God's work. Jesus was rejected by the Pharisees because in their paradigm if Jesus were the Messiah, He would hang out with them and do things their way. Instead, Jesus hung out with sinners and did things God's way. In Matthew 15 we see the Pharisees traveling to Jesus to criticize Him for not teaching His disciples to follow their traditions. The word "break" in verse 2 above means literally "to walk alongside." A modern equivalent could be "to sidestep or to skirt." Thus they asked Jesus, "Why do your disciples sidestep our traditions?" Jesus then wisely answers a question with a question, using the same word and asking, "Why do you sidestep the commands of God through your traditions?" He then exposes the system (or traditions) that the Pharisees had created that allowed them to ignore the needs of their parents, thus violating the commandment to honor and obey. Jesus further condemns it as not just sidestepping the fifth commandment but nullifying it.

The Pharisees' traditions expressed their paradigm. A paradigm is the set of assumptions behind our traditions. Traditions are the infrastructure that supports our paradigm. To deal with paradigms we must be willing to take a good hard look at our traditions. We must be willing to ask some hard questions about our assumptions. Even now some of you may be uncomfortable because some of these ideas are pushing on your beliefs and practices. You may even be critical because these ideas may conflict with your view of church. Let me encourage you to continue reading and don't give up on me yet. If what we believe is truth, it will stand up to all interrogation; if it is not truth, it will, as in this passage, not stand up to questioning and be exposed for what it is. Let it go.

GIVEN THE TEACHINGS OF JESUS IN MATTHEW 15, CONSIDER THE FOLLOW QUESTIONS:

Should all traditions be eliminated?

Of course not. Traditions are often benign practices that have meaning to some while others can take them or leave them. At times some traditions are helpful to the gospel and can be used missionally to reach people groups. Missionaries will often engage the traditions of a culture in order to earn respect and the right to be heard.

What is one criterion for evaluating my traditions?

We need to evaluate traditions by their effect on the Gospel and the Word of God. We should always be willing to give up traditions that *sidestep* or *nullify* the Word and the movement of God. As people of The Book, the Bible should be the most important filter by which we critique our traditions and practices.

Could we be engaging traditions or practices which presently nullify the movement of God?

Traditions and the paradigms they support are assumptions. They are like ruts. We fall into them and move where they lead without thought. In them comfort becomes complacency, routine becomes ritual, interpretations become theology, and practices become pomp and pageantry. In order to keep traditions alive, some groups will add an air of mystery so that the traditions become an end in themselves with power conveyed through their practice. At times these traditions are seen as so powerful that they can convey power apart from faith and surrender. Thus, you can live like you want as long as you regularly practice the traditions. No, I am not talking about the Catholic Church; I am talking about evangelicals. I am talking about my tribe of Baptists. I have moderated meetings, consulted in conflicts, and seen churches split because of traditions. In 30+ years of ministry, I have never seen a church split due to theological issues. I have, however, seen churches fall apart because of the conflicting traditions of various paradigms.

How important is it for us to evaluate our traditions in light of Scripture? How often? By what means?

Traditions should regularly be evaluated in light of scripture. The questions we should ask of every tradition and the paradigm it supports are:

Is it biblical?

Although Christendom stands on the shoulders of great men whose teaching should be considered as we study the Word, we should never forget our primary source of all faith and practice is the Bible. We should always be willing to ask, "Is this belief, practice, and/or tradition scriptural? If so, what does Scripture say about it?" We must always be willing to challenge, in light of biblical truth, the orthodoxy that comes from our local church, denomination, past and present writings of great men of God, and, yes, even our historical church fathers and early church councils. Again, I am not saying that just because we determine some things to be traditions that they should be eliminated. I am saying that they do need to be identified for what they are with a willingness to let them go if necessary.

Does it violate scripture (unbiblical)?

This question applies to the violation of specific commands and prohibitions found in scripture: "Thou shalt not... or Thou shalt." Some things are clearly NOT right and good and we should not do them while some things ARE good and right and we should do them. What is important to understand is that

> ...worshiping only the true God stops us from wasting our time, energy, and resources on false, non-existent gods that cannot meet our needs.

any commands are for our good. As parents set rules to protect their children, God has established rules to protect us from our own stupidity. For example, not worshiping any other god but worshiping only the true God stops us from wasting our time, energy, and resources on false, non-existent gods that cannot meet our needs.

Is it scripturally neutral?

Some people might believe that everything we do has to have a biblical precedent, and if it is not in Scripture, we should not do it.

John 8:31-32 To the Jews who had believed him, Jesus said, "If you hold to my teaching, you are really my disciples. 32 Then you will know the truth, and the truth will set you free."33 They answered him, "We are Abraham's descendants and have never been slaves of anyone. How can you say that we shall be set free?"34 Jesus replied, "Very truly I tell you, everyone who sins is a slave to sin.

According to this passage, before you and I were Christians, we were slaves to sin and, thus, not free. Slave are subject to their masters, limited in their choices, and, therefore, not free to try new things. As disciples and followers of Jesus, we have the capacity to know truth that sets us free. This freedom means that we can now try new things within the context of biblical truth. Christians and churches are free to try new things personally and corporately. Biblically neutral means, simply, that it does not violate biblical truth and is okay to try. "If it is not unbiblical, unethical, or immoral, we may try it" was a phrase I often used with my church to move them away from unbiblical, ineffective traditions and toward being more relevant and missional. On some level, God has restored His creation so that we as Christians are now free to explore, gain knowledge, and subdue the earth, as well as expand God's kingdom.

Is it effective?

Does it move people toward God and His purposes for their lives? On some level we have to consider effectiveness as an evaluation of our traditions in light of biblical truth. I am not referring to the effectiveness of biblical truth itself; I am referring to the effectiveness of our application of biblical truth as expressed in our traditions. As we apply God's word, we must consider results. For example, in the area of evangelism and kingdom expansion, consider this truth: the kingdom of God is expanded only when people are accepting Christ, as seen through a public profession of faith in baptism. In other words, baptism is the sign of kingdom expansion.

I know of a church that in one year grew by about 400 people. This seems wonderful until you realize that only about 8% or 30 people became part of the church through baptism. The rest of the growth was from swapping sheep with another congregation in the area that had been experiencing trouble. On the other hand, I know of a church plant that in a year baptized over 100 people, which was more effective when it is it evaluated by the biblical truth of the Great Commission (Matthew 28) to make disciples.

In addition, as we look at the Great Commission, we are commanded to teach believers to obey all that Jesus commanded. We are called not just to teach but to teach to OBEY, not just to teach to obey but to teach to obey ALL that Jesus commanded! We cannot read this without feeling some pressure to not just be faithful but also be fruitful, not just committed but productive, and not just efficient but effective.

EVALUATING YOUR TRADITIONS

Let's apply this to ministry today. Let's take a good look at some of our practices and traditions and evaluate them in light of the New Testament. List below practices, teachings, and traditions of your church or church experience. Include expectations that are written and unwritten. What are the assumptions of others concerning ministry and leadership? What does a pastor do from week to week? What is expected of him? What practices make up the Sunday Service? What is the expected weekly schedule of the pastor or leader of the church? Examples might be: passing the offering plate, pastoral visitation to membership, congregational singing.

_____   _____

_____   _____

_____   _____

_____   _____

_____   _____

Now go back to the list and place a "T" by items you would consider Tradition and an "NT" by items you would consider New Testament practices and theological must-haves.

Below I have produced a list in which some items are traditions of the church and some are New Testament practices. This list is for discussion and consideration, not condemnation.   Of those that you may label as tradition, some are missional and assist in the Gospel but may need to be dealt with at a later date if they become ineffective. Do the same as above with my list. How would you label the following? "T" or "NT"?

_____ Only the ordained can baptize and oversee Communion
_____ Sunday order of service
_____ Personal prayer and Bible study
_____ Group prayer and Bible Study
_____ Worship
_____ Wednesday Night Prayer meeting
_____ Sunday Church Service
_____ Pulpit Preaching: one to many lecture style of preaching
_____ Pulpits, pews, steeples, church buildings
_____ The idea of clergy and laity
_____ Ordination as spiritually authorizing by church leaders
_____ Ordination as affirming by church leaders
_____ Suits, ties, choir robes, and clergy uniforms
_____ Seminary trained leaders

_____ Pastor-led weddings and funerals
_____ Visitation

I know this is redundant, but please hear me when I say that I'm not espousing eliminating any of the traditions you see in the list above. That is not my desire. What I am saying is that we need a clear understanding of what is truly scriptural and what we have incorporated through our traditions. In my day, Wednesday night prayer meeting and Bible study was standard practice, yet it is not specifically mandated in scripture. It doesn't mean it's wrong to meet to pray on Wednesday night, but neither is it wrong not to meet on Wednesday night. Yet some churches have split over the removal of such traditions that might have been deemed ineffective and thus needed to be discarded. I myself have moderated meetings as Christians fought over such traditions. What I found to be ironic is that in many cases, non-active members will show up at a business meeting to fight for traditions that they have not personally engaged in years. Wow! Tradition is a powerful thing.

> In order to change our paradigms, we must have a clear understanding of what we might need to let go of and what we need to hold onto.

Once again, my desire in producing this list is that we have a clearer understanding of what needs to be evaluated, challenged, and addressed in order to move forward with and have a movement of God. Our paradigm is made up of many traditions and common practices. In order to change our paradigms, we must have a clear understanding of what we might need to let go of and what we need to hold onto.

CHPATER 4

PARADIGM SHIFT: *SHIFT TO WHAT?*

Now, a paradigm shift not only means we need to move away from something, it also means we need to move toward something else. It is a shift, not a stop. So the question is *what are we shifting to?* The answer is found in looking back to the New Testament church. Many pastors and leaders say they want a New Testament church, but they are unwilling to evaluate, challenge, and even remove traditions that stand in the way of creating a new paradigm. So allow me to submit to you a list of characteristics that I think describes the New Testament church we all desire.

THE NEW TESTAMENT CHURCH WAS REACTIONARY AND RESPONSIVE TO THE HOLY SPIRIT.

The big commandment in Acts 1 is not in verse 8 but in verse 4; it was not "go and be witnesses" but "wait on the Holy Spirit and you shall be witnesses." The Acts of the Apostles was more the Acts of the Holy Spirit and the reaction of the Spirit-filled individuals. As you read the book of Acts,

> ...for every action of the Holy Spirit in the world, there was an equal and corresponding reaction of Spirit-filled people.

you will notice that the disciples continually reacted to the work of the Holy Spirit more than they initiated His work and leaders were facilitators more than instigators. In Acts 2, a loud noise got the attention of a city filled with devout followers of Judaism. A light show led them to the Spirit-filled apostles, who, seizing the opportunity, presented the

Gospel supernaturally in their native languages, and 3000 surrendered to Christ. At Pentecost, the Holy Spirit did the work.

Throughout the book of Acts, for every action of the Holy Spirit in the world, there was an equal and corresponding reaction of Spirit-filled people. Like a dance, they followed as the Spirit led. Is this not the way the church should function today? All the strategy and planning in the world could not create the Pentecost of Acts 2, the crowd that gathered at the healing of the lame man in Acts 3, the Samaritan Pentecost of Acts 8, and the Gentile Pentecost in Cornelius' home in Acts 10. All this came from obedience to one command in Acts 1: not Acts 1:8 but Acts 1:4, not to "be witnesses" but to "wait" on the Holy Spirit. The greatest surfers cannot make a wave; the greatest weathermen cannot make the weather. Likewise, the greatest preachers cannot make a movement of God.

This Spirit indwelled and directed all believers to do great things for God, many of whom were unnamed. We all know the big names in Acts, the Apostles, Peter, James, John, Paul, and Barnabas, but we must realize that it was unnamed Spirit-filled believers who started the church in Antioch that became the hub of Paul's missionary journeys to the Gentiles. We are the spiritual descendants of these unnamed Spirit-led men and women. Named or unnamed, any Spirit-filled believer can see and respond to the Spirit and be a part of a movement of God.

THE NEW TESTAMENT CHURCH WAS REVOLUTIONARY.

If I understand the word "revolution" correctly, it means *to replace the present system of authority with a new one.* In the days before the Normandy invasion, there were people behind German lines who were sending crucial information about German troop movements to the Allies in anticipation of the

Allied invasion. While Germany would call them traitors and probably shoot them, we would call them heroes and revolutionaries. Similarly, Christians are behind enemy lines and are called to do this same thing—to revolt against the present kingdom of darkness and replace it with the kingdom of light. We are called to seek first God's Kingdom (Matthew 6:33) and to pray for His kingdom to come on earth as it is in Heaven (Matthew 6:10). Literally, we are to pray for an invasion. Sounds like a revolution to me.

The Jews were looking for a revolution and revolutionary leaders. They were looking for a David-like Messiah who would lead them to overthrow Rome and set them up as the ruling class of the world. Jesus fought against this paradigm His whole ministry. It is what is behind passages like *"Jesus, knowing that they intended to come and make him king by force: (John 6:15 NIV)* or questions like *"Lord, are you at this time going to restore the kingdom to Israel?" (Acts 1:6 NIV)*

Of course, the revolution that Jesus leads is against sin and all its comrades and consequences. After Pentecost the Holy Spirit opened the minds of the disciples to this truth, and they became consumed with advancing God's Kingdom in the hearts of men. They believed that through the Good News of Jesus Christ (the Gospel), the present regime of self, sin, and Satan

> ... Christians today do not understand that when they became followers of Jesus, they did not join a club but became part of a revolt.

would be overthrown and replaced with God's Kingdom in the hearts of man. They were so passionate about their revolutionary cause that they gave up all, even life itself, for it. Many Christians today do not understand that when they became followers of Jesus, they did not join a club but became part of a revolt. All Christians are revolutionaries who should be praying daily for an invasion: *"Your Kingdom come, your will be done, on earth as it is in heaven." (Matthew 6:10 NIV)*

THE NEW TESTAMENT CHURCH WAS SIMPLE.

Simple message

John 3:16 For God so loved the world that he gave his one and only Son, that whoever believes in him shall not perish but have eternal life. (NIV)

This is not rocket science. The perfect God loves imperfect humanity and through Christ has provided a way to forgive and restore our relationship to Him. This is the gospel; it is good news. In Acts it was simplified in phrases such as Paul's response to the salvation-seeking Philippian jailer: *"Believe in the Lord Jesus Christ and you will be saved"* (Acts 16:31 NIV). God made becoming a Christian easy; He did all the work and made its message simple, too.

Simple practices and meek symbols of our faith

Picture this at the end of a meal. Someone picks up a cup of what everyone is drinking and the bread that everyone is eating and says, "These represent my sacrifice for you." Simple, to the point, no pomp, no pageantry, just a simple meal and simple symbols. In Acts we are told that the disciples broke bread in homes. Did this mean that they ate dinner together or took the Lord's Supper together? Well, yes - both! If they did it as Jesus did, after eating a meal together, someone would point out that all of this would never be possible without the sacrifice of Jesus. The response was, "I will eat and drink to that." Now we know, like so many things man gets his hands on, practices such as this get corrupted and are either over-endowed or undervalued.

Simple focus

The focus of the New Testament church was to make followers of Jesus and to teach them to know and experience His transformational Word, thus becoming more like Christ Himself. This was done with a simple formula: go, baptize, and teach.

THE NEW TESTAMENT CHURCH WAS NATURAL/ORGANIC/INSTINCTIVE.

Acts 1:4, 8 (NIV) On one occasion, while he was eating with them, he gave them this command: "Do not leave Jerusalem, but wait for the gift my Father promised, which you have heard me speak about... ...8 But you will receive power when the Holy Spirit comes on you; and you will be my witnesses in Jerusalem, and in all Judea and Samaria, and to the ends of the earth."

Acts 1:4 naturally led to Acts 1:8; waiting on the Spirit naturally led to being witnesses. As a matter of fact, it was assumed by Jesus that the 120 who waited for the Holy Spirit would be witnesses in Jerusalem, Judea, and Samaria and unto the ends of the earth. The disciples were not witnesses because they had been informed or educated; they were witnesses because they experienced life with Christ. In other words, their witnessing was a product of their experience. Often there was not even a plan to be a witness. They were surprised by the opportunities presented by the Holy Spirit.

In general, the whole idea of being a witness precludes planning or strategy. Witnesses are created out of situations and circumstances that they have observed and experienced. Without observation

Going is easy and natural for those who are being.

and experience, you cannot be a witness. People don't create events they are witnesses to; it just happens to them.

The disciples would have been liars to deny what they had

seen and experienced in Christ, and it would have been cruel to not let others know that they could experience it, too. "This Jesus whom you crucified, God has raised from the dead" was a truth that could not be denied but instead must be shared. What they had witnessed and experienced transformed them and made sharing it easy, instinctive, and natural. Likewise, if we have truly experienced transformation as a result of our continual relationship with Christ, it will be easy, instinctive, and natural to share that experience with others. In other words, we should not just be hearers and doers of the Word; we should be "be'ers" of THE WORD (namely, Jesus Christ). Being like Christ in our relationship to God is the goal of Christianity. Going is easy and natural for those who are *being*.

THE NEW TESTAMENT CHURCH WAS RELATIONAL.

Matthew 22:37-40 (NIV) Jesus replied: "'Love the Lord your God with all your heart and with all your soul and with all your mind.' 38 This is the first and greatest commandment. 39 And the second is like it: 'Love your neighbor as yourself.' 40 All the Law and the Prophets hang on these two commandments."

How can we not make relationship top on our list when Jesus Himself tells us that the greatest commandment is to love God and the second is to love others? The gospel is all about restoring humanity's relationship to God and others. If you could flip a switch and in an instant the world would follow the Great Commandment of love found in Matthew 22:37, it would literally be heaven on earth. In the New Testament Church love was the theme. They didn't just give to the Gospel cause; they gave to one another. Their newfound personal relationship with God produced such a love for each other that many of them sold some and some of them sold all to meet the needs of their brothers and sisters. Acts 2 tells us that in the NT church believers had such intimate relationship with one another that they had all things in common and no one had needs that remained unmet. As a parent presently living with adult children, I can tell you that this is hard to do. While my adult children want all things in common, my wife and I are pushing for all things separate, starting with separate houses. Of course, I am joking, but at least for me it does make a point. While I have great kids who, thankfully, are all seeking and serving the Lord and we all have a great relationship with each another, I do not know if it compares to the relationship the Spirit created where they had all things in common. I am amazed that the Spirit in the NT church could achieve something among strangers that equaled or even exceeded family relations.

THE NEW TESTAMENT CHURCH WAS PERMEATING.

Luke 13:20-21 (NIV) Again he asked, "What shall I compare the kingdom of God to? 21 It is like yeast that a woman took and mixed into about sixty pounds of flour until it worked all through the dough."

The church of the New Testament was not about an outward, counter-cultural change, a political movement, or an overt operation. It was far more of a covert operation that permeated the culture. Jesus describes the Kingdom as God as being like yeast that starts with a little and spreads throughout the dough. This doesn't mean the change the church makes in the world is not outwardly evident and immense: it is. The church should have an expansive impact on its environment, just like the obvious effect that yeast has on dough, making the difference between a cracker and a loaf of bread. This change infiltrates from the inside out. In the

NT church, transformed individuals were like yeast that permeated its environment and transformed it, winning the lost and creating churches.

THE NEW TESTAMENT CHURCH WAS TRANSFORMATIONAL.

In Matthew 13:1-23, the *Parable of the Sower* is all about transformation. In this parable, the seed (the Word of God), planted in good, cultivated soil (the heart) that is not hampered by hardness, shallowness, or distractions will be transformed and will produce something completely different – a tree, fruit, and more seeds.

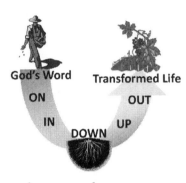

Again, Romans 12:2 tells us that Christians should stop conforming or allowing themselves to be conformed by the world and instead be transformed by a new way of thinking. Transformation is a major purpose of the church.

People were changed when they encountered the New Testament church. People who became believers are described in scripture as changing spiritual states, moving from unrighteousness to righteousness, from darkness to light, and from an enemy of God to a friend of God. Men gave up their professions to become "professors" of Christ. In Acts fishermen became fishers of men, Peter the denier became Peter the preacher, and Saul the persecutor became Paul the missionary. All of this indicates transformation had taken place.

> **Men gave up their professions to become "professors" of Christ.**

THE NEW TESTAMENT CHURCH WAS VIRAL AND HIGHLY COMBUSTIBLE.

In the New Testament church, the Gospel, like a virus, was highly infectious, and Christianity was caught more than taught. Knowing that Jesus had never been to Antioch, it is interesting that the word "Christian" was first used there to describe the disciples who acted just like the one they were talking about. This church at Antioch became the mission center for Paul's missionary journeys.

In addition, like coals in a fire, the gospel was combustible. When a coal rolls away from a fire, it will do one of two things: it will either start a new fire or go out. Persecution that scattered the early church in Jerusalem became the catalyst for church planting. If the people of your church were scattered today, would the flame go out or would it start new ones?

THE NEW TESTAMENT CHURCH WAS AN INVESTMENT.

Acts tells us that people sold some or all they had and gave it to the church. They never considered it a loss but a gain to give all. Giving to the church was an investment in the Kingdom of God on earth. Do Christians in the church give with the same attitude? Is the average church member confident that their investment will yield great returns, expanding and benefiting the Kingdom of God, thus positively impacting the world?

Is what the typical church spends money on a kingdom of God investment? Remember, the New Testament church that expanded its influence throughout the Roman Empire did it with no one investing in buildings, programs, or many of the things we spend money on today. The NT church invested in God's kingdom, for His glory, not man's.

THE NEW TESTAMENT CHURCH WAS LARGE AND SMALL GROUP ORIENTED.

Acts 2 tells us that these new followers of Jesus heard the Apostles' teachings in the temple and met in homes to discuss it. There was an equal emphasis on large and small groupings. The NT church was not just a forum for a preacher to preach; it was also a place for people to dialogue. It had an equal emphasis on small group fellowship, accountability, nurturing, and teaching.

THE NEW TESTAMENT CHURCH WAS INFORMALLY EDUCATED, BUT BOLD NONETHELESS.

Acts 4:13 (NIV) When they saw the courage of Peter and John and realized that they were unschooled, ordinary men, they were astonished and they took note that these men had been with Jesus.

The New Testament church was led by informally educated men. The educated were amazed at the confidence and understanding of the followers of Jesus. The NT church valued and evaluated leadership far more by character than knowledge and education. In Acts 6 the criteria for choosing leaders was not education but a spirit-filled reputation. They were to choose men who were "known to be full of the Holy Spirit and wisdom" (Acts 6).

> Love is not rude, but love can be offensive at times.

These Spirit-filled men were bold but not abrasive. They offended but did not seek to offend. Love is not rude, but love can be offensive at times. We are to speak the truth in love.

A true movement of God requires our availability more than our ability, more our surrender to God than our joining forces with God, and more of the Spirit of God than the intellect of man.

HOW DO OUR MODERN DAY CHURCHES MEASURE UP?

The big question today is: How does TODAY's church compare to this list? Is there a need for a paradigm shift? Does the church today need to take a good hard look at traditions and remove some that are obstacles to the movement of God? Most of us, especially those who have been in ministry for any length of time, would not describe the church as responsive to the Holy Spirit, revolutionary, infectious, or simple. We would not describe the majority of Christians who inhabit the church as bold or highly invested, nor would we say their faith is infectious. While some see a need for change of some sort, mostly limited to methods and models within the same paradigm, others see the need for a whole new paradigm. The purpose of this section is to point out the need for something different, not in the message itself, but beyond method and models to an entirely new paradigm.

The questions at this point become more personal:

- Are you interested in seeing a NT type of movement of God?
- Are you willing to challenge traditions and give up old paradigms if necessary?
- Are you willing to be a doer of the truth God reveals?
- Are you willing to consider some ideas that are outside your present paradigm?

If you answer "yes" to any of these questions, I encourage you as a pastor of an existing church, as a layperson, or as a potential or present church planter to read further as we explore the Transformative Church Planting Movement. As the writer I do not presume to have all the answers for you. I really expect to create more questions for some readers. This is not a prescription where you can take two pills and call me in the morning; it is far more like the blue pill and red pill that Morpheus offered Neo in *The Matrix*. Take the red pill and stop reading and stay where you are, or take the blue pill and keep reading and you may enter a painful new reality, a new paradigm. Being middle aged at 55 (because I plan to live to 100), I do desire to invest the rest of my life in seeing a movement of God. I believe God in His sovereignty has orchestrated my life, giving me experiences that have prepared me for such a day as this. I also believe that by His grace I can be a part of something much bigger than myself.

In the next sections, we will seek to understand the nature of the Transformative Church Planting Movement, the biblical foundation for it, and the basic fractal that permeates it at each level. We will then move on to how to create a TCPM, beginning with your sphere of influence, and explore how it grows and reproduces.

CHAPTER 5

UNDERSTANDING TCPM

Why call it Transformative Church Planting Movement? What is the biblical basis for it? What is the basic fractal or component that makes up the TCPM? These are questions that will be addressed in this section.

DEFINING TRANSFORMATIVE CHURCH PLANTING MOVEMENT

What is TRANSFORMATION?

Romans 12:1-2 (NIV) Therefore, I urge you, brothers and sisters, in view of God's mercy, to offer your bodies as a living sacrifice, holy and pleasing to God—this is your true and proper worship. 2 Do not conform to the pattern of this world, but be transformed by the renewing of your mind. Then you will be able to test and approve what God's will is—his good, pleasing and perfect will.

Think of our bodies as the tool of life. My body is the instrument of my soul, my life. What I do with my body is a reflection of my soul. In this verse we are to offer our bodies, the instrument of life, as a living sacrifice. This sacrifice is to be holy, set apart, different from the world we live in. This pleases God. Verse 2 tells us that this is a process of transformation. Like clay in the potter's hands, we are continually being pressured to be conformed and molded by the world into the image the world desires. Instead, we are to be changed from within (metamorphosis), transformed as God changes the way we think. As God works from within changing the way we think, it will change the way we perceive the world, which

> Transformation means that we know, see, feel, act, and are more like Christ.

35

changes the way we feel, which, in turn, will change the way we act in our bodies.

The greatest measurement of a church is not how big we are but how many people are being transformed, not how many people come on Sunday but how many transformed people are launching out on Monday. Transformation means that we know, see, feel, act, and are more like Christ. I have chosen to use the word "transformative" in Transformative Church Planting because I believe it is the adjective that should describe everything we do. In the Great Commission we should go to transform, we should baptize to transform, and we should teach to transform. This is the making of a disciple.

What is a CHURCH?

A church is a community of followers of Jesus Christ of no particular size that is fulfilling the Great Commission motivated by the Great Commandment. These followers study the Word to be transformed, both individually and in groups, and participate together in the practices of baptism and the Lord's Supper as reflections of their faith.

What is church PLANTING?

A church plant is new body of believers as a result of disciples being made in a local area and organized for the purpose of fulfilling the Great Commission motivated by the Great Commandment. Church planting is a result of evangelism. After being scattered by persecution, the disciples did not go to plant churches. They went out to share the Good News. As they did, people responded and were organized into churches.

What is a MOVEMENT?

move ment (moov'mənt) n. 1. A series of actions and events taking place over a period of time and working to foster a principle or policy: a movement toward world peace. 2. An organized effort by supporters of a common goal: a leader of the labor movement.

Most movements move from the bottom up. They start at the grassroots level and then grow. They start with an individual who surrounds himself or herself with individuals who share a passion and desire for change. Of course, they feel

> **A movement is like a virus or contagion; it is small, reproduces quickly, permeates, and transforms.**

that the change is significant and needful. Also, movements cannot be programmed. To have movement we must think in terms of a wave that becomes a tsunami. We must think of multiple generations and extended family, not necessarily a bigger family--many small interconnected units, not one big one.

A movement is like a virus or contagion; it is small, reproduces quickly, permeates, and transforms. The New Testament church was like this. Pliny the Younger, governor of Pontus and Bithynia from 111-113 AD, wrote to Emperor Trajan concerning Christians in his region:

*I therefore postponed the investigation and hastened to consult you. For the matter seemed to me to warrant consulting you, especially because of the number involved. For many persons of every age, every rank, and also of both sexes are and will be endangered. **For the contagion of this superstition has spread not only to the cities but also to the villages and farms.***

God created Christianity to be a continual movement. In Matthew 13:31–33, Jesus is describing the power of the one or the little to create a large movement.

Matthew 13:31–33 (NIV) He told them another parable: "The kingdom of heaven is like a mustard seed, which a man took and planted in his field. 32 Though it is the smallest of all your seeds, yet when it grows, it is the largest of garden plants and becomes a tree, so that the birds of the air come and perch in its branches." 33 He told them still another parable: "The kingdom of heaven is like yeast that a woman took and mixed into a large amount of flour until it worked all through the dough."

Like a seed, it takes only one single individual to create a movement that benefits many, or like yeast, it takes only a small amount to have a big impact. Once again, I remind you that yeast is the difference between a cracker and a loaf of bread.

Movement is implicit in the Great Commission (Matthew 28:19). In it we are commanded to make disciples through the process of going, baptizing, and teaching. I used to see this as cyclical, but, more correctly, it is an ever-expanding spiral, like a tornado with an ever-growing vortex expanding as it moves upward. Jesus' "teaching them to obey all I have commanded" sends us right back to the commandment to go and make a new generation of disciples who will then go and make disciples. In Acts 1:8 Jesus says that the Spirit empowers disciples to become an ever expansive  influence to "Jerusalem, Judea, Samaria, and to the ends of the earth." It is a command to transform others, teaching them to transform others.

Most people would not describe the church today as a movement. The questions we need to ask are, "Why not? What stops the church from being the movement God intended?" The answer may be in what stops movement in general. Think about it. Any hard, solidified, or established object will slow, or, if it is big enough, stop movement. Spiritually, immovable objects can take the form of the following:

* Traditions – patterns of behavior that are repeated over time and have meaning to those who practice them

- Institutionalism – systems and traditions that are organized for efficiency
- Monuments such as buildings—when the church is described more as a building and less as people
- Nostalgia – feelings from the past sometimes brought on by the practice of traditions
- Business – Over-emphasis on money and budgets
- Preservation of past eras and experiences
- Teachings of the "sainted," or any local church's "early church fathers"

Given this list, the questions we should ask are: "Are there traditions, systems, physical attachments, nostalgic feelings, dependencies, past people or events, or popular teachings that are preventing the movement of God? Is there anything in my life more important than seeing a movement of God in my world?"

CHAPTER 6

BIBLICAL BASIS FOR TCPM

Three key passages form the basis for the five characteristics of the transformative church planting movement. These passages describe the Motive, Mission, Magnitude, Means, and Method of the Movement.

MOTIVE OF THE MOVEMENT: LOVE FOR GOD, THEN OTHERS

Matthew 22:37-40 (NIV) 'Love the Lord your God with all your heart and with all your soul and with all your mind.' This is the first and greatest commandment. And the second is like it: 'Love your neighbor as yourself.' All the Law and the Prophets hang on these two commandments.

"Love" has such a broad meaning. I can look at my wife with loving eyes and say, "I love you," and then look at the Little Debbie Nutty Bars on the table and say, "I love them." In all the marriage counseling I have done, I have sometimes wondered if the love the couple is talking about is more "Nutty Bar love" than real love. Love from Jesus' perspective could be described as a self-sacrificing affection for another that places their real needs and legitimate desires above my own. This describes the love of God for us and the motive that brought Jesus from heaven to earth.

In the Great Commandment found in Matthew 22:36-40, we also see the priority of love: it is God first, and then others as self. As Christians we understand love for God as most important because God first loved us and sent his Son as the payment for our sins (1 John 4:9-10). It is this love for us that gives us the definition by which we can understand love and thus love God in return and others as ourselves. I have many friends whom I love so much that I might die for them, but I do not know one of them for whom I would give up one of my children. Giving up one of my children would be giving ALL. God gave ALL in Christ for us, and He asks of us no more than He was willing to give us – ALL! Understanding and experiencing God's love for us prepares us to love Him with all our being, and this relationship provides the security by which we can love others.

MISSION OF THE MOVEMENT: MAKE DISCIPLES

*Matthew 28:18-20 (NIV) All authority in heaven and on earth has been given to me. Therefore go and **make disciples** of all nations, baptizing them in the name of the Father and of the Son and of the Holy Spirit, and teaching them to obey everything I have commanded you. And surely I am with you always, to the very end of the age.*

It is sad that in America there are many people who call themselves "Christians" but there seems to be few true followers of Jesus; there are many churchgoers but few disciples. There are many who work for the Lord but neglect their personal relationship with the Lord of the work. The word "Christian" can be used to describe right-wing conservative political groups or left-wing liberal social reform groups. For many, "Christian" is closer to a description of what they are not than what they are; "I'm a Christian" means I am not Islamic, Buddhist, Hindu or a member of any other world religion.

The primary verb in the Great Commission is "make disciples." The word means "to make a follower of." When the disciples heard this term, they must have thought in terms of Jesus the Rabbi and His calling to follow Him. They must have remembered leaving their nets (Peter, Andrew, James and John), tax collection tables (Matthew), and causes (Simon the Zealot) to follow Jesus. These men changed professions to become followers of Jesus: fishermen became fishers of men and a tax collector a writer of the gospel. A disciple or follower of Jesus was one who surrendered all to be a life-long learner of Jesus Christ, was transformed by His word, was becoming more like Jesus, and was compelled to help others do the same. This is the mission of TCPM.

MAGNITUDE OF THE MOVEMENT: JERUSALEM, JUDEA, SAMARIA, ENDS OF THE EARTH

*Matthew 28:18-20 All authority in heaven and on earth has been given to me. Therefore go and make disciples of **all nations**, baptizing them in the name of the Father and of the Son and of the Holy Spirit, and teaching them to obey everything I have commanded you. And surely I am with you always, **to the very end of the age**.*

*Acts1:8 But you will receive power when the Holy Spirit comes on you; and you will be my witnesses in **Jerusalem, and in all Judea and Samaria, and to the ends of the earth**.*

> **...as long as there is one lost person in the world, MY church should grow and reproduce.**

The highlighted areas in the passages above describe the magnitude of our mission. We are to engage every nation with the Gospel until the end of the age (possibly a reference to Christ's return). We are to do it from Jerusalem, which in application might be considered where we are right now, to the ends of the earth. Needless to say, the magnitude of our engagement with the Good News is immense.

Allow me to help you understand this another way by asking a question. "How big should any church be?" or "When should a church stop reaching and growing?" The answer is: as long as there is one lost person in the world, MY church should grow and reproduce. My church should reach people, grow, and reproduce until Christ returns and until all have heard the message.

On an additional note, in Acts 1:8, the word "and" means that we should be doing these simultaneously: "Jerusalem, and in all Judea and Samaria, and to the ends of the earth." We should always have one foot in our community and one in the ends of the earth. This is a good argument for giving and participating in missions and, for my tribe, participating in the Cooperative Program.

MEANS OF THE MOVEMENT: THE HOLY SPIRIT

*Matthew 28:18-20 All authority in heaven and on earth has been given to me. Therefore go and make disciples of all nations, baptizing them in the name of the Father and of the Son and of the Holy Spirit, and teaching them to obey everything I have commanded you. **And surely I am with you always**, to the very end of the age.*

*Acts 1:4-5, 8 On one occasion, while he was eating with them, he gave them this command: "Do not leave Jerusalem, but wait for the **gift my Father promised**, which you have heard me speak about. For John baptized with water, but in a few days you will be baptized with **the Holy Spirit**... ...8 But you will receive power when the **Holy Spirit** comes on you; and you will be my witnesses in Jerusalem, and in all Judea and Samaria, and to the ends of the earth.*

Nothing important can be done for God without the Holy Spirit. If He is not present in what we are doing, it is only a product of man's talents and ability, and the effects of it will probably last only a lifetime at best. *And surely I am with you always* can be a confusing statement when you realize that Jesus ascended shortly after saying it, unless you understand it as a reference to the presence and deity of the Holy Spirit. The Holy Spirit in us is the same as Jesus' presence with us.

In addition, 1 Corinthians 2:10-16 indicates that the Holy Spirit is God's personal spirit that He shares with us. No other religion teaches the idea of God inhabiting man like Christianity does. This brings me to ask: how is it then that the ever-present, all-powerful God, who created and sustains all things, seems to be absent from

> **The Holy Spirit is the leader; we are middle management at best.**

or impotent in many of the churches in America and that Christianity, as a whole, is losing influence, turning America into the 4th largest mission field in the world?

I would submit that the missing component is the Holy Spirit, and without Him the motive is not felt, the mission is not achieved, and the magnitude is never reached. The Holy Spirit is the means, the glue that ties it all together. As stated in the previous chapter, the Holy Spirit is the catalyst of God's work on earth; we are just facilitators. He is the initiator and instigator; we are the managers. He is the leader; we are middle management at best.

METHOD OF THE MOVEMENT: GO TO BAPTIZE, BAPTIZE TO TEACH, TEACH TO GO

*Matthew 28:18-20 (NIV) All authority in heaven and on earth has been given to me. Therefore **go** and make disciples of all nations, **baptizing** them in the name of the Father and of the Son and of the Holy Spirit, and **teaching** them to obey everything I have commanded you. And surely I am with you always, to the very end of the age.*

While the primary verb forms the mission (to make disciples), the participles "go," "baptize," and "teach" form the method. We cannot make disciples without going to them as Jesus came to us (Ph. 2), without baptizing them into a community of supportive believers, or without teaching them to obey the teachings of Jesus. These three things form the method of making a disciple and are fleshed out in the ministry of Jesus and the book of Acts. Go, baptize, and teach also form the basic fractal of the Transformative Church Planting Movement that we will discuss in the next chapter.

CHAPTER 7

THE BASIC FRACTAL OF TCPM

Think not of what you see but what it took to produce what you see.

-Benoit Mandelbrot

Benoit Mandelbrot is known as the father of Fractal Geometry. While traditional geometry could be used to measure, describe, and create manmade structures and buildings, it could not measure or describe God-made structures like mountains and clouds and living organisms like trees and plants. While traditional geometry could measure things with straight lines and geometric shapes, it could not measure roughness and jaggedness. Mandelbrot's work introduced the world to a new kind of geometry that could now measure such things.

Loren Carpenter, a young computer programmer, discovered Mandelbrot's work in the 1970's and used it to create the first computer animated images that became the foundation for CGI (Computer Generated Images) in movies and video gaming today. In a day where all animation was hand-drawn, Loren Carpenter, while working for Boeing, discovered that he could take a basic shape or fractal, like a triangle, and duplicate it repeatedly to produce complex irregular shapes, thereby animating landscapes and mountain ranges on his computer. Because of his innovative use of fractals, he was hired by George Lucas and later became the Co-founder and Chief Scientist of Pixar Animation Studios.

The following triangles illustrate this idea of fractals. In the first diagram you have a triangle, and as you connect the center point of each line that makes up the triangle, you create more triangles within the first. Now, as you connect the center points in each of the smaller triangles, you create more triangles and so forth. Notice that the small triangles are just like the large ones: fractals.

Fractals are non-regular geometric shapes that have the same degree of non-regularity on all scales. In other words, no matter where you look on the structure, large or small, you will see a similar pattern repeated. Fractals surround us in natural things such as snowflakes, trees, leaves, and clouds. Consider the images below and the similarities between the whole and the parts.

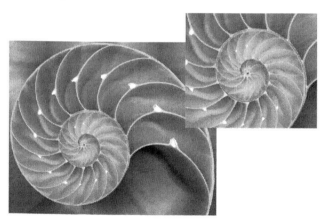

I know your question is, "What does any of this have to do with the church?" The answer is more obvious when you apply the idea of fractals to God's creation and living organisms. Fractals in living organisms are similar structures that move from small units to large units, from single cell to multi cell units. They also are reproductions of self-same structures with smaller units structurally supporting larger units. This is why a small sprout from an acorn looks like and can structurally become a large oak tree (see the image below).

In church work, we would say that the basic fractal of the church is the individual believer. We even call the church a body because it is made up of bodies (fractals). As the individuals in a church change, the church will change. You cannot have corporate transformation without personal transformation. While many may agree with this truth, the methods for achieving individual transformation can be quite different. Today the most common method is still large to small—corporate to individual. We do corporate events such as crusades, revivals, and Sunday services, seeking a response from the individual. We build buildings to gather large groups and create events hoping for individuals to respond in faith.

This is what is often called an attractional model. It starts with the large and moves to the small. We create events with a plan to gather many and then organize them. Crusades, revivals, and conferences are major parts of the activity of the church, all designed to attract people, bring them in, get them saved, and plug them in. Sunday services are worship events designed to attract people; once we get them in, we will develop them. Seminary trained me to expand the organization and then fill it. What they did not teach me is that just expanding does not fill it. Creating or expanding an organization does not always produce a vacuum; sometimes it just creates empty space. Creating new ministries does not always create new opportunities to minister. I am not criticizing this model, just saying it may be incomplete.

Please do not hear me say that this model is bad. I am a product of this model. I am a Christian today because at the age of nine I gave my heart and surrendered my life to Jesus during the invitation of a corporate gathering. I surrendered to the ministry as a product of the same methodology. Most of us who know and serve Christ today are products of the corporate to individual model. I am not questioning its effectiveness in the past but perhaps its effectiveness in the present in bringing individuals to faith in Jesus, spiritual maturity, and discovery of missional purpose. In our present American culture, I believe we need to focus more on the individual and on smaller units.

Many churches and church plants today want to focus on Acts 2 as the model for church planting and church growth. At Pentecost Peter preached, and 3000 became committed followers of Jesus. They began to meet in small groups in homes where they fellowshipped and discussed the teachings of Christ taught by the Apostles. As they did, their lives became transformed, demonstrated by their devotion to one another, desire for others to hear the Gospel, and significant giving (sometimes all) to the church family for ministry. All of us would love to see Acts 2 happen over and over again. We want to start with 3000 and then organize them to grow and go.

ISSUES WITH THE ATTRACTIONAL MODEL

I would suggest four issues with our present paradigm of starting and growing churches. There may be more, but time constraints will focus our attention on these.

Issue #1: It's costly.

My first concern, as I see it, is that in our efforts to duplicate Pentecost, we are using manmade ways. I am not suggesting that manmade ways are wrong in and of themselves; I am asserting that they are costly. In our efforts to recreate Pentecost, we create big events, produce big concerts, organize big need-meeting conferences, and build big new buildings. Every year we may attempt to create an Easter event in hopes it will become a modern Pentecost. With sincere hearts we want to gather lost people, proclaim the Gospel, and make followers of Jesus. Then we plan to organize them to grow and go. "Go" often means "Go and invite your friends to our next big event" or "Join a team to help with the next big event."

All of this has one big problem: it requires a lot of resources up front. The attractional model requires considerable money, people, energy, and talent at the outset, and we need a full-time staff person (church planter) to organize it. In my present ministry, putting a full time church planter on the field and giving him enough resources to get started would require $75,000 to $100,000 just for the first year, probably less if he is single and willing to live on Ramen Noodles and peanut butter or if he has a wife with a good job. Most times support from outside the church plant (from a denomination or other churches and organizations) has a shelf life of only 3 – 5 years. I myself have, at times, been driven by the need to replace decreasing funds from outside support with contributions from inside the church plant (from members). It's very tempting to begin to focus on finances over ministry, which could lead to compromises of value and vision. Additionally, because of the people resources that being attractional demands, we may at times empower individuals based upon talent more than spiritual maturity. This shortsighted selection and advancement of immature individuals will often lead to long-term problems and conflict.

What I have seen over the past several years is that the more pagan and removed from Christianity our world becomes, the less likely new members are to come in as substantial givers. Turning followers into good stewards takes a lot of time. In addition, many people of today are turned off by seeing money going to indirect ministries such as buildings. This is seen more vividly when you get out of the Bible Belt into emerging areas where people are removed from the church and its influence.

God is gracious, and while this model still works at times and while we rejoice in these successes, the truth is everything I've read, every conference I have been to, and my personal observation tells me we are falling way behind in reaching the lost. If money is the key, we are not at the right door. If full-time church planters, big events, and buildings are the forefront of our church planting movement, we are destined to stay well below the increasing curve of lostness. There's just not enough money. But there is another way.

> **If money is the key, we are not at the right door.**

Issue #2: How you reach them is how you keep them.

No cruise ship would financially stay afloat if it attracted passengers by promising to meet their needs and desires and assuring them the vacation of their dreams and then halfway through the trip began to expect them to do laundry and look after other passengers. What people sign up for is what they expect, and if they do not get what they signed up for, they may jump ship or, worse, choose another cruise liner. This can be true of the attractional model for churches. Having attracted individuals through need-based ministries such as children's ministry, youth programs, concerts, and conferences, it may be difficult to begin to get them thinking in terms of being on mission. Moving people from consumers to producers is not impossible but can be difficult for an attractional church.

Issue #3: It *may* neglect the Holy Spirit's work.

Another thing that might be missing in our present attractional model of starting and growing churches is the work of the Holy Spirit. Although Pentecost was an attractional model, it was the Holy Spirit who made it attractive. A loud noise turned heads and got people's attention. A light show brought onlookers to the disciples who presented the Gospel to them in a culturally sensitive way, with every person hearing in his own language. 3000 became followers of Jesus, were added to the church, and started the process of growing as Christians. Again, in Acts 3, Peter and John, through the power of the Holy Spirit, healed the lame man, which attracted a crowd. Again Peter shared the Gospel, and another 3000 became followers of Jesus and were added to the church to grow and go.

Today, maybe as a result of our revivalist heritage, the attractional model is the primary approach or paradigm for starting and growing churches. It is the Field of Dreams approach. If we build it, they will come. If we preach it, they will come. If we sing it well, they will come. With technology we produce visuals and sounds to turn heads and get people's attention. Don't get me wrong, I love new technology because it has helped me in many areas of life and ministry, but it will never replace the supernatural work of the Spirit and the transformative word of God.

Issue #4: Quality must precede quantity.

In the Acts 2 model, it appears that quantity preceded quality. Although I do not believe this is true and will address it later, it is a major part of our paradigm.

First of all, it must be understood that quality and quantity are not opposed to one another. I have actually had pastors (whose churches have not grown in years) tell me, "We are into quality not quantity" as if this excused their lack of reaching the lost. On the other hand, I have had young church planters so driven by numbers that their self-esteem would rise and fall with each Sunday's attendance. I once had a young church planter, after launching a second campus, tell me he was disappointed and thinking about shutting the second campus down because there were only 200 to 300 people in average attendance.

Quality and quantity are not mutually exclusive; as a matter of fact, we often want both. For example, I do not want to fish all day and catch one big fish, nor do I want to fish all day and catch a bunch of little fish. No, I want to fish all day and catch a lot of big fish; I want quality and quantity. Furthermore, no youth leader comes home from camp and says to the parents, "I know we took ten kids to camp, but due to the dangers at camp, we were able to bring home only seven. Let me assure you, however, that they are the best and brightest of the bunch." No, we want all ten kids home safe and sound; we want both quality and quantity. God expects faithfulness (quality) and fruitfulness (quantity) from us. In addition, God is into giving a lot (quantity) of great things (quality). God wants all the world the world to be saved. When we look at the New Testament, the question is: "Where did it all begin? Did it start with quality or quantity?"

> **In the New Testament, quality preceded quantity. Acts is the sequel to Luke.**

In the New Testament, quality preceded quantity. Acts is the sequel to Luke. If you did not see the first movie, you will probably not fully understand the second. In Luke and the rest of the Gospels, we see Jesus' ministry as foundational to the events of Acts. We also see that Jesus was focused more on the quality of His followers than the quantity. At times He often seemed to discourage potential recruits. On one occasion, when two individuals presented their resumes and expressed a desire to follow Him, He responded with a job description that seemed to include homelessness and abandonment.

John 8:18-22 When Jesus saw the crowd around him, he gave orders to cross to the other side of the lake. 19 Then a teacher of the law came to him and said, "Teacher, I will follow you wherever you go." 20 Jesus replied, "Foxes have dens and birds have nests, but the Son of Man has no place to lay his head." 21 Another disciple said to him, "Lord, first let me go and bury my father." 22 But Jesus told him, "Follow me, and let the dead bury their own dead."(NIV)

After feeding 5000 in John 6, Jesus' popularity soared, and His following grew until the middle of chapter 6 when He exposed their real motives for following Him. They were seeking food, not His teaching. He then challenged them to join in His suffering, to "eat his body and drink his blood." The truth is that they were not willing to see beyond the metaphors, for upon hearing this challenge, they retreated back into their own worlds. At the end of chapter 6, all who were left were the Twelve. Over and over again, Jesus used strong challenges and metaphorical teachings to raise the bar and test the level of surrender of His followers. Over and over, all but the few failed to advance to the next level.

The closer Jesus got to the cross, the smaller His following. The week of Jesus' death began with His Triumphal Entry into Jerusalem with the multitude chanting, "Hosanna! Blessed is he who comes in the name of the Lord! Blessed is the king of Israel!" (John 12:13) and ended with only His mother, a few women, and John watching Him die. After three years of ministry (His death, burial, resurrection and ascension), we find in the first chapter of Acts 120 highly committed disciples, the largest church in the Gospels. But with 120 Spirit-empowered believers, Christianity expanded from Jerusalem to Rome.

I would submit to you that quality precedes quantity—specifically, that the quality of the ministry of Jesus produced the quantity of Pentecost. The Gospels (life and teachings of Christ) were the foundation for Acts. Acts would have not taken place without Luke. Jesus had one who leaned on Him

(John), three He took special places (Peter, James, John), twelve He called Apostles, seventy He called disciples, and 120 praying in the upper room who became filled with the Holy Spirit.

THEN.... 3000 who became His followers at Pentecost (Acts 2), 3000-5000 who became followers after the healing of the lame man (Acts 3), and finally the spread of the gospel throughout Jerusalem, Judea, Samaria, and to the ends of the earth (The Book of Acts).

Without the foundation Christ built in the calling and training of the Twelve, the 3000 at Pentecost never would have taken place. Even after Pentecost, when persecution scattered the disciples, they did not go to build buildings and fill them; they did not even go to plant churches. No, the disciples went and made other disciples who then organized into churches. In light of this, could it be that what we do in the individual and the few may be the beginnings of a movement of many? Does the church need to spend more time transforming individuals and less time growing the organization? Is there a need to focus on the micro (the smallest fractal unit) because it makes up the macro?

The need of church planting is to think small, in quality organic fractals that can grow and reproduce, quickly supporting the larger movement. Transformed individuals, making up transformed groups, making up transformed churches, making up transformed networks, produce a movement. The basic fractal of TCPM is the individual who becomes a follower of Jesus experiencing transformative relationships, a learner of Jesus experiencing the transformative Word, and an influencer for Jesus experiencing a transformative calling. Having experienced this, he or she will go, baptize, and teach others who will do the same and so on and so on.

CHAPTER 8

THE BASIC FRACTAL OF TCPM: GO TO BAPTIZE, BAPTIZE TO TEACH, TEACH TO GO

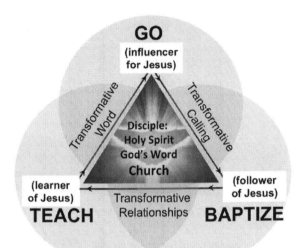

What is the basic fractal for the NT Church? What is found in individuals that is duplicated and multiplied exponentially? What transforms individuals that transforms groups that transforms churches, regions, states, and nations? What is the mustard seed that grows into a tree where people from every nation of the world can perch and rest (Matthew 13:31-32)? The answer is found in the method of the Great Commission. To make disciples we must go, baptize, and teach or *go to baptize, baptize to teach,* and *teach to go.* Jesus did this for you and me. Jesus came (go) to baptize, He baptized to teach, and He taught to go. The basic definitions of each of these aspects of the fractal are as follows.

Go to Baptize:

This part of the fractal describes an influencer for Jesus who is now going on mission to make followers for Jesus. To go to baptize, we need to experience a Transformative Calling. When we experience transformation, it will produce a driving message and mission. Good news is easy to share.

Baptize to Teach:

This part of the fractal describes bringing a person into a deeper relationship with Christ and other believers. A major part of this is Transformative Relationships. Christianity is more caught than taught, more modeled than just manufactured, more organic than industrial, and more family-equipped than institutionally developed. Becoming a disciple starts with a commitment to Christ and His community (through the act of baptism).

Teach to Go:

This part of the fractal describes the person who is engaging the Transformative Word, experiencing the mercy and grace of God, and becoming an influencer for Christ. Like the seed in Matthew 13 that falls on well-cultivated ground and is allowed to run its natural course, the Word will transform and produce abundantly. Through the Word of God, a life unencumbered by hardness, shallowness, and distraction will be transformed and will naturally reproduce.

WHAT HAPPENS WHEN ONE OF THESE ASPECTS IS MISSING OR OVER-EMPHASIZED?

Academic Church

The academic church exists to educate. Some churches focus all their attention on going to get them, bringing them in, and educating them. They *go to baptize* and *baptize to teach* but are weak in the area of *teach to go*. James tells us that we are not just to be hearers of the word; we are to be doers of the word. Jesus said to whomever much is given, of them much will be required (Luke 12:48). Spiderman's Uncle Ben said, "With great power comes great responsibility" (Ok, I am a fan). With the academic church, the fractal is incomplete because there is little or no emphasis on *teach to go*.

Churches often fall into this model because it is the model for conveying information in our colleges, seminaries, and big churches with popular preachers and authors. Seminaries are filled with students ready to learn more, but not only do they take the information into their ministry, they take the academic model, too. I know what this feels like. I can name professors whom I loved to listen to. I came out of seminary thinking that if I preached it (like them), people would come. To me small groups were important but were secondary to my preaching. I existed to educate, and my assumption was the more they knew, the more they grew. The problem was that while it was an efficient method of conveying information, it wasn't necessarily effective. One of my great frustrations was preaching to the same people over long periods of time, sometimes years, and seeing no change, no transformation.

A second reason we fall into this academic model is that we want to emulate popular preachers and authors without any regard for the hard work that got those preachers where they are today. We preachers love to listen to and want to be like great preachers, but the problem is that we see only the tip of the iceberg. We do not see what it took to get these men to the top of their game. Often for most of these men, it took a lot of one-on-one ministry. They learned how to pour their lives into individuals, making new followers, learners, and leaders. As we listen to these men on our iPhones or read their books, we do not see the organization around them that God has used them to build. I am always disappointed when I hear a young preacher say, "I just like to preach. I don't like to pastor or counsel." What I hear is, "I do not like to get my hands dirty in the soil of the hearts of individuals." Unfortunately, this kind of ministry is destined to limited effectiveness because the old adage really is true: "People do not care what you know until they know you care."

Club Church

The club church exists to sustain resources such as buildings and membership. They do outreach only as their resources are threatened; therefore, at times they may be good at *go to baptize* and *baptize to teach* but will be very resistant to *teach to go* unless going is defined as helping inside the walls of the church. These types of churches often memorialize people and things, and they love to get together. Unity is their top priority, and they will resist anything or anyone who might threaten it, even if it is a biblical movement of God. This church would say, "If we cannot move together, we just won't move!" So they DON'T!

Numbers Church

The numbers church exists for numbers. They are great at *go to baptize* but will often neglect the challenges that may come with *baptize to teach* and *teach to go*. It is about fellowship but not necessarily relationships. "How many did you have Sunday?" is the most important question. Ministry stands or falls based on numbers of attendees, not on effectiveness.

It is important to note at this point that the basic fractal of TCPM is all about making influencers for Jesus who will go to baptize, baptize to teach, and teach to go. Church is not an end but a means, a conduit, a channel. Sundays exist for Mondays through Saturdays, and the people of the church exist to be missionaries in their home place, work place, and play place. The church and its leadership exist to send and *equip the saints for the work of ministry* (Eph. 4)

THE BASIC FRACTAL STARTS WITH YOU!

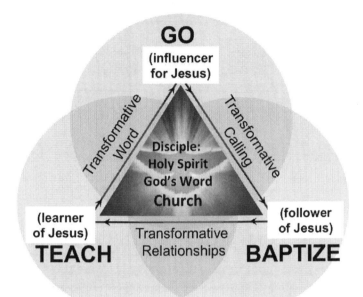

We have for years attempted to encourage people to go, witness, and share their faith with others. Most methods for doing this focus on behavior. Evangelism Explosion, Continuing Witnessing Training, and Share Jesus without Fear are good training tools for the person who has experienced transformation and is ready to develop some practical skills in witnessing. These trainings are great for those who want to go, but most Christians don't. Most Christians have not experienced transformation in such a way that they are compelled to share their journey with others.

This is why the basic fractal that is the building block and cornerstone for Transformative Church Planting Movement begins with you experiencing Jesus and the work of the Holy Spirit as a follower, learner, and influencer. Remember, this is what Jesus did with His disciples, turning fishermen into fishers of men. He came (go) to baptize, making them followers. He then taught them as learners and made them into influencers who would then go themselves and make followers, learners, and influencers.

Are you a(n)…

- **Follower of Jesus** experiencing a transformative relationship with God and others, exhibited by physical baptism as a symbol of following Christ in a community of believers?

- **Learner of Jesus** experiencing the transformative Word, exhibited by reading, studying, and active participation in a learning, accountability community?

- **Influencer for Jesus** experiencing a transformative calling, exhibited by Christ-like character produced through the Word, the Holy Spirit, and a biblical community?

This follower (learner) who becomes a leader and influencer is now ready to *Go*.

CHAPTER 9

GO TO BAPTIZE: TRANSFORMATIVE CALLING

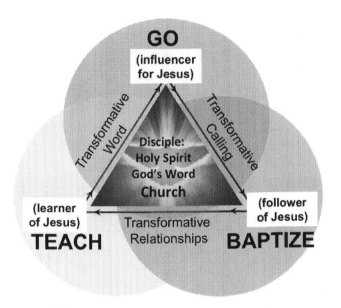

Again, the prerequisite for *go to baptize* is a transformed life that produces a transformative calling to see others transformed. Are you experiencing life with Jesus in such a way that it compels you to help others experience transformation? Is your life a transformed life ready to transform lives? We are called to pass it on. According to the scriptures below, what we have received from God, we are to freely give away. We have experienced comfort from God to comfort others, we have experienced reconciliation with God to bring reconciliation to others, and we have experienced teaching from God to teach others.

2 Cor 1:3-4 Praise be to the God and Father of our Lord Jesus Christ, the Father of compassion and the God of all comfort, 4who comforts us in all our troubles, so that we can comfort those in any trouble with the comfort we ourselves receive from God.

2 Cor 5:17-21 Therefore, if anyone is in Christ, the new creation has come: The old has gone, the new is here! 18 All this is from God, who reconciled us to himself through Christ and gave us the ministry of reconciliation: 19 that God was reconciling the world to himself in Christ, not counting people's sins against them. And he has committed to us the message of reconciliation. 20 We are therefore Christ's ambassadors, as though God were making his appeal through us. We implore you on Christ's behalf: Be reconciled to God. 21 God made him who had no sin to be sin for us, so that in him we might become the righteousness of God.

2 Tim 2:1-2 You then, my son, be strong in the grace that is in Christ Jesus. 2 And the things you have heard me say in the presence of many witnesses entrust to reliable people who will also be qualified to teach others.

While the attractional church expects people to leave church excited and go to their home place, play place, and work place inviting others to come to hear the Gospel, the transformative church relies on the attractive nature of transformed individuals to open the door for the Gospel. Having experienced real

> ...the transformative church relies on the attractive nature of transformed individuals to open the door for the Gospel.

transformation, this transformed individual is compelled to share his story with others out of sense of urgency and calling.

Characteristics of a Transformative Calling

A transformative calling is a calling of a transformed life to transform lives. Again, through Jesus' sacrifice and by God's grace, if we have really experienced transformation, if we are different people in Christ, more like Jesus, experiencing the Fruit of the Spirit, people will notice and we will be compelled to share. Peter says we should always be ready to give others a reason for the hope within us. The assumption is they see the hope within us.

What does a transformative calling look like? The transformative calling is made up of two things: servanthood produced by mercy and influence produced by grace.

Servanthood produced by mercy

It was a common practice in Jesus' day for a host to arrange for servants to clean his guests' feet. In Luke 7:36-50, Jesus entered the house of a Pharisee, and as they were eating, a sinful woman came to Jesus and began to serve Him, fulfilling the responsibility that His host should have provided. As she washed His feet with tears and wiped them with her hair, Jesus' host began to criticize Him for allowing this woman to touch Him. Jesus then seized the opportunity to teach His Pharisee host about mercy and its effects on the individual experiencing it. He reminded His host that it was this woman who took on the role of servant and performed the task that the host should have provided. More importantly, Jesus pointed out that she served motivated by her gratitude for the great mercy she had been shown, making the point that where great mercy is experienced, great love is felt and great service is expressed. *Therefore, I tell you, her many sins have been forgiven—as her great love has shown. But whoever has been forgiven little loves little. Luke 7:47 (NIV)*

The foundation of calling is servanthood that comes from gratitude, having experienced the great mercy of God. One point that could be made from this passage is that those who understand and experience great mercy will love and serve greatly while those who feel they are in need of little mercy will love and serve only a little. Where would you and I have been in this story: blind to our need for mercy and judging those experiencing it, or experiencing mercy wanting to serve God and others? This woman, as she was cleaned up on the inside, wanted to get her hands dirty on the outside in service to Jesus.

Mercy is God not giving us what we deserve while grace is God giving us far more than we ever deserve. Although they are two sides of the same coin, they are different. In God's mercy, He forgives me my sins and removes them from my life, and in His grace He gives me a home in heaven. In true discipleship one must experience mercy, then grace. Just like a glass must be emptied before it can be filled, our lives must be purged of bad habits, our hang-ups, in order to be filled with the good things God desires to give. This is the process of sanctification or being made holy by God. How many times have pastors and church leaders empowered the talented only to be embarrassed later by hidden sins? People who experience real house-cleaning kind of mercy from God want to serve Him out of a heart of gratitude. Gratitude and love are the chief motives of a Christian and foundational for a transformative calling.

Influence produced by grace

Just like taking a dirty glass off the table after dinner, placing in the dishwasher for cleaning, and then removing it and placing it in the cabinet makes a glass available for use, God in His mercy cleans us up, and in His grace, He equips us for use. In His mercy, He frees us from sin, but in His grace He frees us to new life. In His grace we have a greater understanding of our spiritual ministry SHAPE--our **S**piritual gifts, **H**eart's passions or desires, **A**bilities and talents, **P**ersonality and temperament, and life **E**xperiences that God can use to help others. These are the things that form our personal transformative calling.

As we trust God, He entrusts us.

Through God's mercy and grace, we understand who we are and what we should be doing for Him and His Kingdom. The more I understand about God and how He created me, the more I understand and trust His investment in my life. As we trust God, He entrusts us. Just like in the parable of the talents, God gives to each according to his abilities. His investment in us shows His confidence in us. One of the sins of the person who hid his talent was that he did not trust the judgment or investment that God made in him in giving him the one talent (Matthew 25:14-30). In essence, this servant was telling the master, "I don't believe you know what you are doing in giving me this talent."

As we take with confidence the gifts or investments of God and invest in others, God will bless. As God blesses, our influence increases. The more we invest what God entrusts to us, the more others see the God-given return and the greater our influence. In the Bible, the faithful followers of God were often given great influence in their community. Abraham was feared and respected as a prince even though he was a nomad in the land. Joseph through faithfulness was recognized and given authority in Potiphar's house and later in Pharaoh's kingdom. David, the faithful shepherd boy, became King David, the greatest king of Israel. In addition to this, 2 Corinthians 15:20-21 says that all Christians who have experienced reconciliation are given the ministry of reconciliation and are now ambassadors of God. The title "Ambassador" assumes influence of one country in another. We are called to be God's influence in a lost world, and, as 2 Corinthians 15:20-21 says, 20 *We are therefore Christ's ambassadors, as though God were making his appeal through us. We implore you on Christ's behalf: Be reconciled to God. 21 God made him who had no sin to be sin for us, so that in him we might become the righteousness of God.*

Allow me to share a disclaimer. Influence does not mean that everyone will like us; it just means that as God's ambassadors, we will be noticed. Being salt of the earth and light to the world does not mean that some will not prefer the unsalted earth and unlighted world. The bland and blind may hate or even kill those who try to influence them as salt and light.

When we experience God's mercy, it leads us to be servants, and then in His grace we experience His equipping and investment in us that produce influence. In God's mercy and grace we are transformed and called to be salt to the earth and light to the world. In experiencing God's mercy, we are forgiven servants wanting to do anything God desires, and in experiencing God's grace, we are gifted, desiring to do the one thing God created us especially to do. In other words, it is in God's mercy that we are willing to do whatever God asks of us, and as we do this, we will, in God's grace, find the specific things He has called us to do that truly motivate us and create greater influence. Ephesians 2:1-10 is all about mercy and grace, two sides of the same coin; it concludes with verse 10: For *we are God's handiwork, created in Christ Jesus to do good works, which God prepared in advance for us to do (NIV)*.

CHAPTER 10

BAPTIZE TO TEACH: TRANSFORMATIVE RELATIONSHIPS

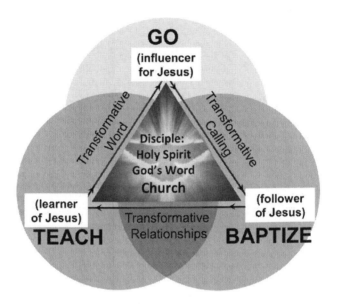

A missionary once said people will better understand Christ when they have a relationship with a real Christian. Relationships are vital to Christianity because Christianity is caught more than it is taught.   If Christianity were a virus transmitted by contact, would anyone ever catch it from their relationship with you?

We need people around us that accept us where we are but are continually encouraging us to move beyond. The key component, then, as we *baptize to teach*, is Transformative Relationships, thus the need for small, intimate settings where we can grow in our understanding of God and one another. These small groups and churches, centered around the study of God's Word, provide a **safe** place where **fellowship, nurturing,** and **accountability** take place.

Fellowship

Years ago, in my ministry to help churches, I created a survey for churches to take a look at themselves. Most churches in decline, especially those that have been in decline for a long time, do not realize that they have unintentionally organized, visionized, and structured themselves to get these declining results. They honestly think that things are good when they are really bad. What usually gets their attention is conflict caused by a pastor or leader who sees things as they really are – BAD—or losses that begin to threaten existence. One of the statements on my original survey reads: *My church has great fellowship.* I noticed that the churches that were in great decline and closest to death would say they strongly agreed with this. What I encountered was a sick view of fellowship. I later revised the survey to clarify what a healthy fellowship was: *My church is great at fellowship. As a result of my church's efforts, I see people building deep, abiding relationships. It is inviting to people who come and visit.* This is *koinonia* fellowship. While fellowship to some means "We get along together such that we can make decisions without significant conflict," biblical *koinonia* fellowship means deep abiding relationships. A person surrendered to transformative relationships is committed to deep friendships where people know him or her intimately and personally, the good, the bad, and the ugly.

Safe Place

In order to have this kind of true, biblical fellowship, a safe place must be created. The group must be like a trash can where all the garbage can go, never to return. It must be like a laundry room where a person can bring his dirty stuff and, through God's grace expressed through others, experience a good cleaning. In order for this to happen, a person must feel that what he shares is kept confidential by the group. He is not being judged but helped. Now, a safe place does not mean a comfortable place. Like trash and dirty clothes, people's problems can be stinky and messy and uncomfortable for them to share and for others to deal with. A safe place is where people are not afraid to feel uncomfortable as they deal with the stinky stuff of life.

Nurturing

When Christopher, my son, was born, I brought him home from the hospital, showed him where all the food was, said, "Son, make yourself at home," and then left him and went to work. NO, I knew better than that... like a good father, I left him in the care of his mother, and then I went to work. LOL

Consider all the times that the New Testament refers to the Word as being spiritual nutrition, the church as being a family, and Christians as being children in a process of growth and development

> **Nurturing that produces growth and maturity happens more in a family atmosphere than in an institution.**

moving toward maturity. Just like a child needs a nurturing environment to be healthy, grow, and mature, a Christian does, too. The problem is that most of us are under the deception that this happens as we get together in large groups in a many to one (congregation to preacher/worship leader) environment. We have trained people to think that just coming and sitting is all or at least most of what we need to be nurtured as Christians. Would this work at home with your children? Of course not!

Nurturing that produces growth and maturity happens more in a family atmosphere than in an institution. It happens living in a community where size is conducive to discussion and interchange; where questions can be asked and answered in a timely fashion; where interruption is welcomed and where the goal is not what I am teaching but what they are learning. A nurturing environment is one where messy lives are revealed and then healed. Once again, we are not told to teach them—we are told to teach them to OBEY. If our methods are not nurturing believers to significant spiritual growth and maturity measured in their becoming more like Christ, we need to evaluate those methods and be willing to give up any method that is not teaching people to the point of obedience. Nurturing requires us to think more like a family and less like an institution.

Accountability

While nurturing means we accept people just the way they are, accountability means we do not expect them to stay there. When Christians fellowship in a safe place where their needs are provided for, accountability is natural. Parents who love their children say NO and take away choices when necessary; they enforce NO through groundings when their children are youth and advise NO and may remove support when they become adults. Just like parents who are not afraid to say NO, Christians should always be ready to hold others accountable, willing to risk fellowship to "speak the truth in love." I find it interesting that one of the reasons my children, who are young adults, fight me when I disagree with their decisions is that they care about what I think. As Christians, we need people around us who care enough about us to state their disagreements with us. We need people around us that when they do disagree with us, it matters so much that it drives us upward in prayer, inward to rethink our position, and outward as we look to others for a greater perspective.

CHAPTER 11

TEACH TO GO: TRANSFORMATIVE WORD OF GOD

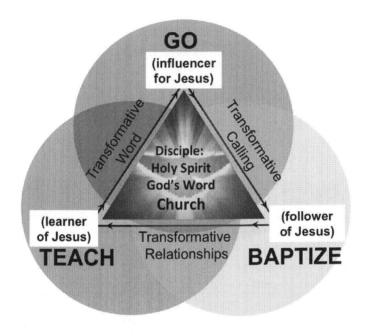

Teach to go is not just about moving a Christian from sitting to serving and from spectating to participating: it implies that the whole purpose of teaching is to **go**. TCPM is not for quitters or sitters. *Teach to go* is a natural part of properly exposing people to the Transformative Word. The Parable of the Sower in Matthew 13 is the model for transformation and forms the core of this belief that God's Word is like a planted seed going on, in, down, up, and out, producing a transformed life people will want to share with others. Working with this model, the TCPM process is adapted to move Christians individually, and in groups, from knowledge to perspective to conviction to competence to character.

TRANSFORMATIVE BIBLICAL MODEL: MATTHEW 13: *PARABLE OF THE SOWER*

In the Bible, transformation is of the greatest importance. Since the fall of humanity, God has desired for man and man has greatly needed to be transformed. As a result of sin, we are separated from a Holy God, and in order to hang out with Him, we must be more than good; we must become something different, a new creation. Think of passages such as Ephesians 2 and Romans 12. Think of all the phrases that imply transformation, such as *new birth, new creation, enemy of God to friend of God, darkness to light, lost to save.*

Throughout the Bible we see examples of people who were transformed. Many times with transformation came a new name: Abram became Abraham, Jacob became Israel, and Saul the "Persecutor" became Paul the "Proclaimer to the Gentiles." At other times there was not a name change, but there was a defined transformation: David the little shepherd boy became David the King, Gideon the "Coward" became Gideon the "Conqueror," Peter the "Denier" became Peter the "Proclaimer," and fishermen became "Fishers of Men." In addition, the lives of Joseph, Moses, and Nicodemus reflect significant transformations. Hebrews 11 is all about faith exhibited in the actions of transformed men and women. The truth is we cannot have a relationship or fellowship with God without transformation from God.

In Matthew 13, the parable of the sower is all about this issue of transformation and how God does it through His Word. Let me remind you that we are commanded to teach followers to obey all the commandments of God. A disciple cannot be made without the teaching of the Word of God that produces obedience which leads to transformation. Read below Jesus' commentary on the parable of the sower.

Matthew 13:18-23 NIV [18] *"Listen then to what the parable of the sower means:* [19] *When anyone hears the message about the kingdom and does not understand it, the evil one comes and snatches away what was sown in his heart. This is the seed sown along the path.* [20] *The one who received the seed that fell on rocky places is the man who hears the word and at once receives it with joy.* [21] *But since he has no root, he lasts only a short time. When trouble or persecution comes because of the word, he quickly falls away.* [22] *The one who received the seed that fell among the thorns is the man who hears the word, but the worries of this life and the deceitfulness of wealth choke it, making it unfruitful.* [23] *But the one who received the seed that fell on good soil is the man who hears the word and understands it. He produces a crop, yielding a hundred, sixty or thirty times what was sown."*

Jesus defines the characters of this story: the farmer, planter, or sower is God, the seed is the Word of God, and the soil is the heart of man. Just like a farmer's expectations of a seed, God expects HIS Word to go on, in, down, up, and out. In other words, when God speaks, His  Word is designed to produce—the product is a <u>transformed</u> life. Or I could say that transformation is the **natural** outcome of God's Word in a prepared (good soil or well-cultivated) heart. When unencumbered by the rocks that prevent roots and the weeds that prevent fruit, God's Word <u>WILL</u> by nature transform a person.

At this point we must ask two pivotal questions:

- While the people of the church are regularly exposed to God's transforming Word, why is the church not transformed nor is it a transforming force in our world?
- Why, in a day of unprecedented resources, abundant tools, and tremendous freedom, is the church in America losing ground?

The answer is found in the individual heart of the believer and then the corporate heart of the church. Jesus says that hearts are suffering from **hardness** or solidification preventing receptivity, **shallowness** or rocks below the surface preventing roots, or competing **distractions** or weeds preventing fruit.

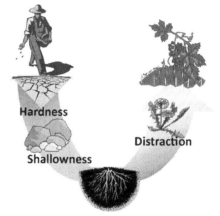

The Transformative Church Planting Movement addresses this issue by getting dirty in the hearts of humanity. Making a disciple requires exposing others to the Word of God and then getting busy in the hearts of others cultivating, digging rocks, and pulling weeds. We must be prepared to address the hardness that comes from ignorance, misconceptions, or at times vain rituals and traditions. We must be willing to go deeper, addressing the issues illuminated by the Spirit of God through the Word of God. We must be willing to confront wrong priorities and misplaced values that distract people from bearing the fruit of the transformed life. Transformation is the work of the Holy Spirit, working in concert with a willing heart in community of believers.

TRANSFORMATIVE PROCESS

The transformative process is where the rubber meets the road. Knowledge leads to perspective, which leads to conviction, which leads to competence, which leads to character. In regards to God's word, as we encounter it, God

wants us to know what He knows, to see as He sees, to feel as He feels, to do what He does, so that we are as He is, not gods but godly children of our Father, living worthy of the name we have been given by grace – Christians. This process permeates every sphere of an encounter, from the individual to the group, for the purpose of moving people from knowing to doing to being. This process works with the Holy Spirit as individuals read the word of God and as Christians learn to rightly handle the word of truth from knowledge through application to incorporation into character. It is holistic, integrating the head (intellect) and heart (passions, emotions, and desires) and the hands and feet (behaviors).

The process is more inductive, probing with questions, than didactic, lecturing. TCPM leaders are trained to use probing questions that move Christians forward into a deeper walk with Christ exhibited in Christ-like character. Leaders seek to discover how participants feel about what they know and see from God's word, what they are going to do about it, and how they see it as changing their lives. Throughout the process, those involved seize opportunities to engage God in prayer for greater understanding, deeper insight, and stronger conviction/brokenness. They also seize opportunities to hold one another accountable for specific strategies for becoming more like Christ.

In addition, the old saying is a true of TCPM: "Feed a man a fish, feed him for a meal; teach him to fish, feed him for a lifetime." The goal is not just to do the process with participants but also to train them to do it for themselves anytime and anywhere they encounter God's word. Just like parents raising children and giving them more and more responsibility, the process places more and more of the burden of discovery, development, and deployment on the Christian himself. The leader should bring less and less to the table while the learner should bring more and more. There is a place where if individuals are not coming to the table having read, meditated, and prepared to share, there is no need to meet.

> ...it is not about what I am teaching but what they are learning that matters most.

Finally, this process is learner-centered instead of teacher-centered. A major paradigm shift for leadership in churches today is that it is not about what I am teaching but what they are learning that matters most.

Our churches are full of individuals who see Sunday as their only significant feeding time, where they are bottle fed from the pulpit a diet of information and prescribed application. What if every Sunday one point from the sermon was taken seriously and incorporated into the life of each individual? What would the church look like a year from now? Yet parishioners go years, even lifetimes, with no significant change. I have used this in preaching to challenge individuals in churches for years, and although it would make a big difference in our churches, it still falls way below what God desires for us. He does not want His children leaving His table with one morsel; He wants them to leave with a full plate that will nourish them and give the strength they need to do the work of the Father.

WHAT DOES THE PROCESS LOOK LIKE?

Knowledge

It begins with knowledge. As Joe Friday from Dragnet would say, "The facts, ma'am, just the facts." Knowledge is about getting the facts correct. It is the lowest level of understanding in any educational model, but it is the first step in making change. We cannot change what we do not know. Right knowledge is the essential first step to right character. However, having knowledge doesn't necessarily mean anything changes. In fact, you can know a lot of good things, things you should do, things that would even benefit you and others, and still be a worthless or even evil individual. Every pack of cigarettes tells the smoker that smoking is killing them, but very smart people still smoke. To us non-smokers, smoking doesn't make sense. It is like traveling down the road and seeing a sign that says, "The bridge is out and if you continue you will die." You would think that this knowledge would cause you to stop and consider another route, but for many, it doesn't. Although knowing the facts does not always equal change, it is the foundation of the process as seen in the diagram above.

These are the kinds of questions and statements that might be used to probe knowledge:
- What are the facts?
- Tell me the story.
- Who are the characters and what did they do?
- Who is speaking?
- To whom are they speaking?
- What is being said?

Perspective

The next level is perspective. In Matthew 13:13-15, Jesus affirms Old Testament prophecy concerning the Jews who would reject Him, saying, "In them is fulfilled the prophecy of Isaiah: 'You will be ever hearing but never understanding; you will be ever seeing but never perceiving.

For this people's hearts have become calloused.'" From this we understand that people can hear the Word and not understand or perceive its meaning because their hearts are hard. Our churches are filled with people who consistently hear the Word every week without changing. Jesus did not speak to inform—He spoke to transform. When knowledge becomes personal, it produces perspective. Perspective is evaluating beyond the facts for the purpose of application. Knowledge looks at what the passage meant while perspective is what it means *to me*.

Once again, this is the work of the Holy Spirit as He takes what I know and helps me to see what it means to me. As I read God's word, He wants me to know more about Him, but He also wants me to know about me and others. Many times knowledge leads to a perspective of all three.

Often the Holy Spirit leads people to different perspectives within the same passage, depending upon their needs. The story of the Woman at the Well tells me about God's love for the outcast sinner. From the woman's perspective, it tells me of Jesus' compassion and intimate, personal love for me and that, even in the midst of my sin, Jesus is willing to meet me. From Jesus' perspective, it tells me about the abundance of ready souls, the urgency to reach them, and the need to pray for God to send laborers. This is where God takes knowledge and shapes perspective that is unique to an individual.

TCPM is not a leaderless movement. We need people who can help with basic understanding and perspective. When the man tormented by lust comes to the group meeting, having read "If your right eye offends you, pluck it out and cast it from you," someone needs to be there to help in understanding how Jesus used metaphors. Someone needs to guide him and help him understand that even a roomful of blind people can still lust in their hearts. It is at this level of knowledge and perspective that we need leaders who are measured by character, not necessarily by education, and who may be in their spiritual journey only a few pages ahead of the other participants. Acts 6 says that leaders should be people who are known to be full of the Holy Spirit and wisdom (not necessarily formally educated). These leaders should guide the individual or group to correct understanding and point them to proper perspective. Knowing and seeing the right things will lead to feeling as God feels.

These are the kinds of questions and statements that might be used to probe for greater perspective:

- What do you see in the passage beyond the facts?
- What does the passage say about God? ...about you? ...about others? ...about all three?
- Who do you identify with in the story? Why?
- What is the most important part of the passage to you? Why?
- What does this mean to you?
- What do you think the Spirit of God is trying to communicate to you though this passage?

Conviction

Conviction is not an ooey-gooey feeling but a deep emotional perspective that comes when knowledge becomes personal. Once again look to my illustration of the smoker. When he attends the funeral of a close friend who died from lung cancer attributed to years of smoking, knowledge not only becomes perspective, but he is also moved by that perspective. If the whole process were a see saw, on one end you would have knowledge and perspective while on the other end you would have competence and character. In the middle, as the fulcrum, would be conviction. Conviction is the pivot point of change and transformation. When a six year old sits beside his father and expresses with tears his fear of losing his father to his smoking habit, knowledge becomes perspective that leads to feeling. This feeling is not to be trifled with because it is a pivotal opportunity to start change.

When we read God's Word, the Spirit is there to convict of God's truth. I would challenge you to look at every major directional change of your life, every big moment, big decision, and big move, and see if they were not punctuated by strong feelings. As Christians we often talk about being broken, moved by the Spirit, and impressed of the Lord. God is not just the God of our minds, He is also the God of our emotions. In fact, denying the way we feel about things is the greatest contributor to ongoing sin.

Over and over in ministry, I have seen the power of emotions. I have seen the sane give in to insanity, the righteous give into unrighteousness, and the dependable and stable become unreliable and inconsistent, all due to the power of emotions. From individuals who have abandoned husbands, wives, children, and church, I have heard statements like, "I deserve to be happy," and "I didn't feel loved." On the other hand, I am thankful for the brokenness of God, how He turns hurts into helps, pain into potential. I am also thankful for the times I have been overwhelmed by His gifts and felt incredible gratitude for His grace. In short, emotions matter and they are pivotal to transformation. We are more likely to change when we feel the heat than when we just see the light.

These are the kinds of questions and statements that might be used to probe conviction:

- How do you feel about what you know and see?
- How do you think this person felt about it?
- Does this passage convict you in any way?
- Does it make you feel grateful, angry, sad....?

Competence

Competence is doing something about what we know, see, and feel. "Practice makes perfect" does not just apply to learning a new skill, it is also literally the way that God transforms us. When we know and see things the way that God  knows and sees them and really feel about things the way that He does, we are compelled to do whatever He desires. As I have seen in my own life, Christians who reach this point and refuse to do and live in what God through the Holy Spirit has revealed are miserable. Like the Children of Israel, they have come to the Jordan River and have seen the land that God has promised, and instead of stepping forward into the Jordan and doing in obedience what they know and see is right, they have chosen to step back and do more research, choosing tents in the desert to palaces in the promised land.

Because some promises of God have an expiration date set by God, what we can do today we may not be able to do tomorrow. Competence is when a Christian seizes the opportunities God gives when He gives them, as Ephesians 5:15-16 says: *Be very careful, then, how you live—not as unwise but as wise, 16 making the most of every opportunity, because the days are evil. (NIV)*

Competence takes the emotions of conviction and does something about them. Although emotions are pivotal, they are incomplete by themselves. Without a plan, what you feel will never be done. We are called to be "doers" of the Word and not just "hearers" (James 1:22). Conviction gives us our best opportunity to do something about what we know and perceive, but if we do not plan to move when we feel like moving, sooner or later we will not feel like moving, so we won't. Illumination of the mind should lead to perspiration in the body.

These are the kinds of questions and statements that might be used to probe competence:
- What will you do with this truth? What will you stop doing?
- Give me your strategy for living in what God has revealed.
- How can we pray for you this week?
- What can I do to hold you accountable for this truth?

The result: Christ-like Character

Consistently doing what we know and feel produces character. Godly character-- Christlikeness--comes from hanging out with Him through prayer and His Word, knowing

83

what He knows, seeing like He sees, feeling like He feels, doing what He does, and being like He is. God has given us the Bible and His Spirit so we might know, see, feel, do, and be like Christ. Jesus never taught for intellectual stimulation; He always taught for transformation, i.e., Christ-like character development.

> These are the kinds of questions and statements that might be used to probe character change:
> - How will it make you more like Jesus?
> - How has this changed you?

IT STARTS AGAIN....THE NEXT GENERATION!

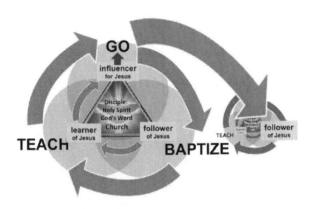

The basic fractal of TCPM, *go to baptize, baptize to teach,* and *teach to go,* starts with me and moves outward. It is not just cyclical; it is an ever-expanding spiral. As a follower of Jesus, who becomes a learner of Jesus and then an influencer for Jesus I now *go to baptize, baptize to teach,* and *teach to go. Go to baptize, baptize to teach,* and *teach to go* is the fractal that everything is measured by.   As an individual I must continually evaluate how I am becoming a deeper follower, greater learner, and more effective influencer for Christ. As I meet with others, I must ask where they are in the process of being made a disciple. Is God sending me to this person to introduce them to Christ (go to baptize)? Am I in their life to model Jesus and help them know Christ and His community better (baptize to teach)? Or am I in their life to help them discover, develop, and deploy for Christ (teach to go)? Furthermore, *go to baptize, baptize to teach,* and *teach to go* is not just for the evaluation of individuals, but every group setting is also appraised by where they are in the process and how or if they are moving forward in the process.

The end result is a Transformative Church Planting Movement that does not measure by size but by sending. It is as interested in quality as it is quantity, as much influencers as followers.   This movement is not just about how many attenders are present on Sunday; it is more about how many missionaries are out there on Monday. As we look on the ripe harvest, we pray with anticipation and with this plan to the Lord of the harvest to send laborers not just **to** the harvest but **out of** the harvest.

CHAPTER 12

TCPM ORGANIZATION

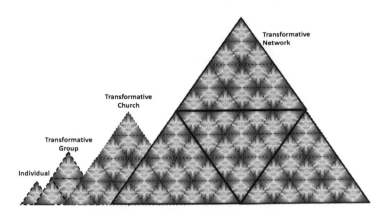

TCPM is organized from small to large and moves people toward the most transformative environment, keeping the basic fractal active and balanced throughout the whole organism from the smallest to the largest.

Transformed Individual

You cannot share what you do not have. The spiral begins with the individual as a follower of, learner of, and influencer for Christ. The next unit entitled *Launching a TCPM* covers the spiritual, personal, and practical steps that an individual needs to take to begin the process. The Work of the Spirit, Accountability, Understanding Your Spheres of Influence, Mapping Your Missional Community, and Starting a Transformative Group are all topics that will be covered.

Transformative Groups

Transformative groups are the most powerful transformational environment. This safe, secure environment is where fellowship is stronger, nurturing is more intense, and individuals are held to the greatest level of accountability. Being gender specific allows for more sensitive topics to be addressed as they are exposed by God's Word. The size of the group needs to allow for significant sharing of the individuals in a reasonable time frame; therefore, a maximum of 6 individuals is suggested. The more people in a group, the more chance of losing the quiet individuals and the more time needed for everyone to share what God is teaching them. Individuals in the group are responsible for reading the assigned or agreed upon passages for the week and using the transformative process to share God's teaching to them.

One facilitator is needed for a transformative group. His or her role is to allow everyone to share what God is teaching them, and he or she is the spiritual guide of the group, always sensitive to the Holy Spirit's work in the lives of individuals and their need for prayer and accountability. The facilitator must be adept at using the transformative process, moving from feeding fish to teaching them how to fish for themselves. More and more, as they meet, the burden of transformation (knowing, seeing, feeling, doing, and being) is placed on the individual. The facilitator is always evaluating the group by the basic fractal, moving them toward going to baptize. Thus, his job is not just to facilitate but also to discover, develop, and help deploy new facilitators to create new transformative groups.

Transformative Church

The Transformative Church is where multiple transformative groups gather weekly in homes or other places to discuss what God is teaching them through their individual reading and transformative group experiences. In the Transformative Church, a meal is shared, the Lord's Supper is taken, the Word is presented, and transformational work in the individual is discussed and witnessed by the group. Leadership exists to guide and facilitate, not to teach and force application. Individuals are responsible for bringing God's transformative work in their life to the group for encouragement, ministry, prayer, and/or accountability. Again, the size of the group is conducive to allow for significant sharing of the individuals in a reasonable time frame; a suggested maximum is twenty people.

Another aspect of the Transformative Church is that it thinks generationally beyond the family to the extended family. The Transformative Church does not exist to get bigger; it exists to reproduce. It is always in a state of change because it is continually moving people through the process of being followers of, learners of, and influencers for Christ. The church then births influencers into new communities who make disciples and start again. The church will also be in a state of change because people that are unwilling to surrender totally to the process of becoming influencers and taking responsibility for their own spiritual growth may at some point stop attending. After much grace and a great deal of patience and tolerance, the Transformative Church is always prepared to let go of the unreceptive who at any level may choose to stop developing. As Jesus said, at times you must "shake the dust off your feet" and move on to those who are moving with God (Matthew 10:14).

Every Transformative Church will need at least three leaders: a Pastor/Facilitator Leader, a Ministry Leader, and a Missional Leader. The Pastor/Leader/Facilitator is the chief leader of the church and the facilitator of the weekly church gatherings that center on the Transformative Word with a goal of teach to go. He is responsible for the Transformative Group Facilitators, and they are responsible to him. Working with the Ministry and Missional Leaders, he will discover, develop, and deploy Transformative Group Facilitators. Ministry Leaders are responsible for developing transformative relationships with a goal of baptize to teach. This leader keeps the church focused on the needs of the group. He or she works with the pastor to create new transformative groups. The Mission Leader is responsible for helping people discover their transformative calling with a goal of go to baptize. He or she also keeps the groups focused on missional opportunities including local, regional, national, and international (Acts 1:8). These three working leaders, with the Transformative Network Leader, will discover, develop, and deploy leadership for new churches.

Transformative Network

A Transformative Network supports and resources the churches; it does not exist to develop programs, campaigns, or slogans for them. It exists to resource them and work with them to help train new leaders and launch new churches and transformative groups. Networks may meet monthly or weekly in events that may look like a traditional church with worship and the proclamation of God's word. They may even through gatherings or other events produce entry points to a relationship with Christ, but they will always move people into participation in transformative churches and transformative groups.

A network will have at least one Network Leader to help with and administrate the ministries of a network. Often he is the core church planter who started the TCPM and raised up the first generation of leaders. He is the leader of leaders, the father of the local movement. Continuing to lead by example, he is the facilitator of a group and church.

CHAPTER 13

CONCLUSION

TCPM is not a new revelation but a synthesis of ideas, readings, conferences, and observations that have spanned my 30+ years of ministry. I believe on some level that churches that are healthy--those that are reaching, teaching, and equipping individuals--are already doing many of the things in this reading. They see the individual and small units as important as or even more important than the corporate gathering. Rick Warren states in his books and conferences that as the church grows larger (in attenders and members) it must grow smaller (in small groups). He even calls his group leaders "pastors," referring to the church-like ministries of these small groups. Years ago, I was exposed to *The Growth Spiral: The Proven Step-By-Step Method for Calculating and Predicting Growth Potential in Your Church* by Andy Anderson. Although the long title still scares me today because it looks like a lot of work, it was a great tool for growing churches and even starting churches. Its principles of growth, training leaders, and reproducing are still valid and needed now more than ever.

This information is nothing new because we've all known these things for a while. It's just time to DO something different. The church in America needs to operate differently, or it will continue to decline much like the churches in Europe, becoming anemic and ineffective, a state that is Christian in name only.

If you are ready to DO something different with this information, the next step is to do the training and launch your own Transformative Group. Be ready to see what God can accomplish through you.

This preview is not a prescription with a preset dosage; it can be used in part or in whole. Take from it what you think will help you expand God's kingdom.

If you have questions or would like to consider moving forward, contact me.

Martin Jones
martinjonesgo@gmail.com
(330) 970-9151

63491890R00057

Made in the USA
Lexington, KY
08 May 2017